Francis Pierrepont Barnard

Strongbow's Conquest of Ireland

Francis Pierrepont Barnard

Strongbow's Conquest of Ireland

ISBN/EAN: 9783337322359

Printed in Europe, USA, Canada, Australia, Japan

Cover: Foto ©Suzi / pixelio.de

More available books at **www.hansebooks.com**

ENGLISH HISTORY
FROM CONTEMPORARY WRITERS

Strongbow's Conquest of Ireland

ENGLISH HISTORY FROM CONTEMPORARY WRITERS.

THE series, of which the present volume is one, aims at setting forth the facts of our National History, political and social, in a way not yet systematically tried in this country, but somewhat like that which Messrs. Hachette have successfully wrought out in France under the editorship of MM. Zeller, Darsy, Luchaire, etc. It is planned not only for educational use but for the general reader, and especially for all those to whom the original contemporary authorities are for various reasons difficult of access.

To each well-defined period of our history is given a little volume made up of extracts from the chronicles, state papers, memoirs, and letters of the time, as also from other contemporary literature, the whole chronologically arranged and chosen so as to give a living picture of the effect produced upon each generation by the political, religious, social, and intellectual movements in which it took part.

Extracts from foreign tongues are Englished, and passages from old English authors put into modern spelling, but otherwise as far as may be kept in original form. When needed a glossary is added and brief explanatory notes. To each volume is also appended a short account of the writers quoted and of their relations to the events they describe, as well as such tables and summaries as may facilitate reference. Such illustrations as are given are chosen in the same spirit as the text, and represent monuments, documents, sites, portraits, coins, etc.

The chief aim of the series is to send the reader to the best original authorities, and so to bring him as close as may be to the mind and feelings of the times he is reading about.

No definite chronological system of issue is adopted, but it is hoped that the entire period of Mediæval and Renaissance history may be covered in the space of two or three years,

F. YORK POWELL,
Editor of the Series.

Ch. Ch., Oxford, 1888

(ENGLISH HISTORY FROM CONTEMPO-
RARY WRITERS)

Strongbow's Conquest of Ireland

Translations from the works of Gerald of Barri, Roger of Howden, Benedict of Peterborough (Richard Fitz-Neal), William of Newbury, Ralph of Dissay, Robert of St. Michael's Mount, Gervase of Canterbury, Ralph Niger, and Gervase of Tilbury, The Archives of Dublin, The Annals of Boyle, The Anglo-Norman Poem on the Conquest known as "Regan," and Extracts from O'Donovan's versions of the Annals of the Four Masters and of the Annals of Innisfallen, Hennessy's version of the Annals of Loch Cé, Mageoghegan's version of the Annals of Clonmacnoise, an English rendering of the Annals of Ulster, Carew's Prose Abstract of "Regan," and other contemporary records.

WITH ILLUSTRATIONS AND MAP

BY

FRANCIS PIERREPONT BARNARD, M.A.,

Head Master of Reading School.

NEW YORK AND LONDON

G. P. PUTNAM'S SONS

The Knickerbocker Press

1888

PREFACE.

"Illa ego sum Graiis olim glacialis Ierne
Dicta, et Jasoniae puppis bene cognita nautis."

THIS little book deals with an event of permanent interest to us It tells the story of the first contact between the newly organized feudalism of Anglo-Norman England and the far older and more primitive civilization of the last independent Keltic states. The period embraced is from A D 1166 to 1186, and the accounts reproduced are taken from the best available original authorities on both sides, including some hitherto unpublished MSS. To the general reader it will not be found wholly uninstructive to read the history of the earliest political connection of England with Ireland.

In the translations an attempt has been made to reproduce the spirit and literary peculiarities of the authors, even though at times the result undoubtedly inclines to the grotesque. What Kingsley said of the old Teuton invaders of the Roman Empire, is true of the mediæval chronicler; in his mental attitude he is like a big boy, half a man, half a child. One must, therefore, in the following pages be prepared to expect deviations from sober history; indeed, the "Expugnatio" of Giraldus Cambrensis, who is by far the most important authority, illustrates this characteristic to extravagance, and is a remarkable farrago of history, poetry, acuteness, credulity, egotism, zeal for the cloth, kinsman-worship, fairness, partiality, good nature, malignity, and pomposity, adorned with a medley of alliteration, conceits, puns, wit, satire, humour, sometimes sheer buffoonery, and now and then downright nonsense. Truly a writer ποικιλόμυθος. With regard to Gerald's excerpts from the classics, even when he is evidently using texts such as we have now, his quotations are frequently not verbatim. Possibly in many instances he relied on his memory, but a considerable number of passages are wittingly altered and adapted without scruple to suit the requirements of the moment. It is necessary to add a word of warning against accepting his personal descriptions as entirely just. Praise or abuse must be discounted according as the character under dissection is that of a Geraldine or not.

There is a class of readers whom I have hoped to secure—learners. Some experience in school work has led me to believe that a short historical "period" or monograph, or a tractate on social economy, forms the best peg on which to hang the extra lessons to which most schoolmasters nowadays devote perhaps a couple of hours a week: hours likely to be none the less profitable and popular because they are not as a rule overshadowed by the looming terrors of a coming examination.

CONTENTS.

		PAGE
	Introduction	7
1166	How Dermot went into exile, and how he was restored to his dominions by the king of the English..	8
1166 or 1167	Of the return of Dermot through Greater Britain	11
1169	The coming of Robert Fitz-Stephen and the taking of Wexford	13
	Of the conquest of the men of Ossory	16
	Another account of the conquest of Ossory	18
	Another account of the conquest of Ossory, *continued*	20
	Defection of Maurice de Prendergast	22
	League of all Ireland against Dermot and Robert Fitz-Stephen	24
	A description of Dermot	26
	How peace was re-established	27
	The coming of Maurice Fitz-Gerald and the reduction of Dublin	28
	Of the preparations of earl Richard	29
1170	The coming of Reimund Fitz-Gerald and the defeat of the men of Waterford at Dundunnolf	32
	The coming of the earl and the taking of Waterford	34
	Of the storming of the city of Dublin	37
	The Council at Armagh	38
	Convocation of the clergy at Clonfert	39
	[Henry II becomes jealous of the success of the adventurers]	40
1171	Death of Dermot, king of Leinster	40
	Overthrow of the Ostmen at Dublin	41
	The speech of Fitz-Maurice advising the sally from Dublin	44
	The sally from Dublin	46
	The treacherous capture of Fitz-Stephen at "The Crag"	48
	A description of the earl	50
	How the Irish fanned the king's jealousy with complaints against Strongbow	51
	Of the meeting of the earl with the king of the English	51
	[Most of the princes of Ireland do homage to Henry II]	53
1171 or 1172	The Synod of Cashel	54
1172	[Henry II winters at Dublin]	58

		PAGE
	First Dublin charter of Henry II	58
	Second Dublin charter of Henry II	59
	Of the storms	60
	Grant of Meath to Hugh de Laci	62
	Letter from pope Alexander III to the Irish bishops	63
	Of the treachery and death of O'Ruarc, king of Meath	64
	The death of O'Ruarc. An Irish account	67
	A description of Maurice Fitz-Gerald	67
	A description of Henry II, king of the English	68
1174	Disastrous incursion into Munster by the earl	75
1174 or	The granting of a bull of privileges by Alexander III	76
1175	[The bull "Laudabiliter" of Adrian IV]	77
1175	The famous storming of Limerick	80
	A description of Reimund Fitz-Gerald	83
	A description of Meiler Fitz-Henry	84
	Roderic pays tribute	85
	A description of Hervey de Montmaurice	85
1176	Relief of the garrison which had been left at Limerick	87
	The speech of Donnell, king of Ossory	88
	Concerning the announcement to Reimund of the death of the earl	90
	[Irish account of the death of the earl]	91
	The burning of Limerick and the burial of the earl	91
	[Gerald's eulogy of his kinsmen]	93
	A description of Fitz-Aldelm	94
1177	Concerning the invasion of Ulster by John de Courci, and the doings of Vivianus the legate	96
	Victory of John de Courci at Downpatrick	98
	A description of John de Courci	99
	Invasion of Connaught by Milo de Cogan	101
	A description of Robert Fitz-Stephen	102
	How peace and order were established in the realm of Ireland by Hugh de Laci	108
	Grant of land by Hugh de Laci to William the Little	110
	A description of Hugh de Laci	111
1178	The two defeats of de Courci in Ulster	103
	Irish prelates start to attend the Lateran Council	105
1180	Death of Laurence, archbishop of Dublin, at Eu, and succession of John Comyn	113
1181	The coming of John the constable and Richard de Pec	112
1182	Assassination of Milo de Cogan : Irish account	105
	Assassination of Milo de Cogan : English account	106

CONTENTS.

		PAGE
1184	The sending of John, archbishop of Dublin, into Ireland	116
	The coming into Ireland of John, the king's son	116
1185	Prince John's Dublin charter	119
	Ale and metheglin customs granted by John to the canons of St. Thomas' Church, Dublin..	119
	[The same confirmed]	120
	Irish account of the administration of prince John	121
	The ill-government of prince John	121
	Of the credit due to Fitz-Stephen, the earl, and the king, and how far they may be acquitted of certain charges	122
	Of the lets and delays to the full and perfect conquest of Ireland	123
	The causes of the untoward events..	126
	Of the three parties among the invaders at this time	134
1186	Assassination of Hugh de Laci: English account	135
	Assassination of Hugh de Laci: Irish account	136
	A defeat of John de Courci	137
	Some results of the conquest	137
	[Conclusion of the Strongbow period of the conquest]	138
	How the Irish race might be completely conquered	139
	How Ireland should be governed	143

Of the character, customs, and external appearance of the Irish	146
Of the matchless skill of this nation in instrumental music	150
Of the villainy and foul duplicity of the Irish	155
Of the axe which they ever bear in their hands, as though it might be a staff	155
Of a strange and monstrous way of inaugurating a king	156
Of the many unbaptized in the island, who have not yet arrived at the knowledge of the faith	157
Of the clergy of Ireland, and how they are praiseworthy in many respects	160
Of a sarcastic retort of the archbishop of Cashel	161
Of a great lake which had a miraculous origin	162
Of the Giants' Dance, which was taken over from Ireland to Britain	164
Of reptiles and the lack of them in Ireland, and how no venomous creatures are found there	165
How the dust of this land is fatal to poisonous reptiles	167
Of the shoe-latchets of Ireland, which are opposed to poisons	168
Of a frog lately found in Ireland	169
Of the isle of Man, which inasmuch as it harbours poisonous reptiles is regarded as belonging to Britain	170
Of two islands, in one of which no one dies; while into the other no living creature of the female sex can enter	171

	PAGE
Of an island one part of which is frequented by good the other by evil spirits	172
Of an island where corpses exposed to the air do not decay	174
Of the wondrous nature of some fountains	174
Of a fish which had three golden teeth	175
Of an island which at first floated, but was at length firmly fixed by means of fire	175
Of miracles, and first of the apples of St. Kevin	176
Of the fleas which were banished by St. Nannan	177
Of bells and staves and other similar relics of the saints	178
Of that most potent relic known as the staff of Jesus; and how a priest was visited with a twofold affliction	178
Of the crucifix at Dublin which spoke and bore witness to the truth	180
Of St. Colman's teal, which are tame and cannot be harmed	181
Of the archers at Finglas who were punished by Heaven	183
Of various miracles in Kildare; and first of the fire that never goes out, and the ashes which do not increase	184
How the fire is kept up by Bridget herself on her own night	185
Concerning the hedge set around the fire, within which no male may go	185
Of an archer who leapt over St. Bridget's hedge and went raving mad; and of another who lost the use of his leg	186
That the saints of this land appear to be of a vindictive disposition	187
Of St. Kevin's gentleness	187
Of the wonderful sanctuaries provided by the saints	188
Of the salmon leap	190
How the salmon leap	191
That the bodies of S.S. Patrick, Columba, and Bridget, which lay at the city of Down in Ulster, were in these our days discovered and translated	192

APPENDIX.

I.	Genealogical tables of the Geraldines and their kinsfolk	193
II.	Lists of the adventurers, royal officers, and others engaged in the conquest	195
III.	Lists of the Irish and Norse chieftains and notables	198
IV.	The Irish episcopate at the time of the invasion	199
V.	Map of Ireland in the time of Henry II, territorial divisions and chief towns	200
VI.	The authorities	202

LIST OF ILLUSTRATIONS

		PAGE
I.	STRONGBOW'S CASTLE OF GHEPSTOW,	*Frontispiece*
II.	MAP OF IRELAND	7
III.	THE ROCK OF CASHEL	54
IV.	SEAL OF HENRY II., FROM ORIGINAL IN BRITISH MUSEUM	68
V.	TOMB OF STRONGBOW AND EVA HIS WIFE IN CHRIST CHURCH CATHEDRAL, DUBLIN	92
VI.	DANISH AXE	148
VII.	MODERN IRISH CORACLE	158
VIII.	ROUND TOWER AT THE ROCK OF CASHEL	163

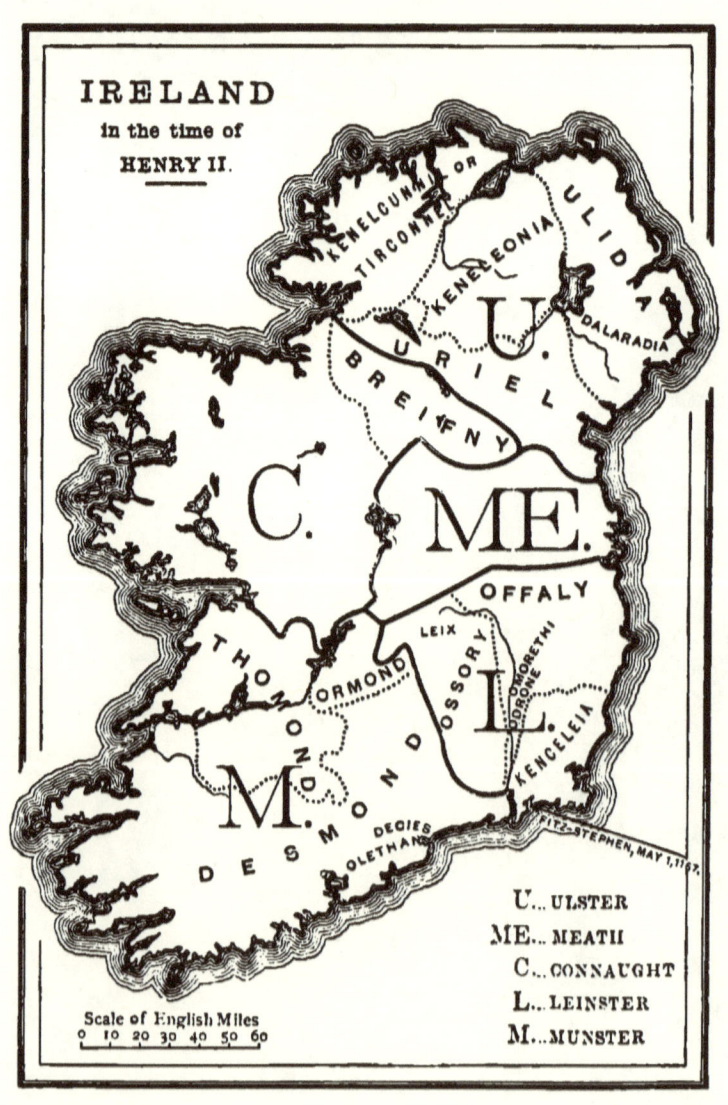

Strongbow's Conquest of Ireland.

[Introduction].

Wilelm. Newburg. Hist. Rer. Anglic. sub anno 1170.

IN considering the history of this land we are at once struck with the following remarkable fact. Whereas Greater Britain, an island like itself lying in the ocean, and at no great distance, has been the scene of so many and such mighty wars, has been so often the victim of the depredations of foreign races, has been so frequently forced to bow the neck to an alien sway, has been taken and held first by the Romans, then by the Germans, again by the Danes, and lastly by the Normans, Ireland was left untouched even by Rome, Rome who extended her dominion right away to the inaccessible region of the Orkneys. Few and faint in the past have been the attacks from outside upon this isle of Ireland. Never did it know subjection, never did it lie prostrate at a conqueror's feet, until the year from the Birth of our Lord one thousand one hundred and seventy-one.*

* * * * *

* When Henry II. went over.

Ireland, like England in days of old, was split up into several states, each with its king, and the whole country was rent by the discord which generally prevailed among them. In proportion as the realm was free from external aggression, so much the more miserably were the natives commonly engaged in tearing the bowels of their fatherland by their intestine feuds.

A.D. 1166.—How Dermot went into exile, and how he was restored to his dominions by the king of the English.

Girald. Cambr. Expug. Hibern. Lib. I. cap. i.

(Dermot, king of Leinster, reigned from 1135 to 1171.)

Dermot Mac Murrough, prince of the men of Leinster, which is one of the five divisions of Ireland, possessed within our times the eastern seaboard of the island, over against Greater Britain, and separated from it only by the sea which flows between. Owing to his youth and inexperience in rule, he became an oppressor of the nobility, and began to tyrannize in a grievous and intolerable manner over the great men of his land. This of itself brought him trouble, which another circumstance contributed to increase; for he eloped with the wife * of O'Ruarc, prince of the men of Meath,† while the latter was absent on a distant

* Devorgilla. This was in 1152, and although it could scarcely have been the immediate cause of the expulsion of Dermot fourteen years later, it possibly laid the foundations of the feud which led up to that event.

† Strictly speaking, prince of Breifny and East Meath. He was nicknamed "monoculus," "the one-eyed."

expedition. 'Fickle and changeable is woman ever,'*
and it is clear that from woman—Mark Antony and
Troy can bear witness to the fact—almost all the
greater evils of the world have come.

King O'Ruarc was heart-struck both by his shame
and by his loss, though he felt the former far more
deeply than the latter, and in the bitterness of his wrath
was bent upon revenge. He forthwith summoned
and gathered together the strength of the neighbouring
tribes as well as his own forces, and aroused to the
same enterprise even Roderic, prince of the men of
Connaught, then high-king of all Ireland. Now the
chief men of Leinster seeing in what straits their
prince was placed, that he was beset on all sides by
the battalions of his foes, began to call to mind their
own claims of vengeance for the grievances they had
long smothered in their breasts; so that being now of
one mind with the enemy they deserted Mac Murrough in this the hour of his misfortune.

Dermot, finding that his resources were falling
away upon every side, that Fortune had turned her
face from him, and that his position was becoming
desperate, after many fierce but unsuccessful en-
counters with his adversaries, at length resolved, as
his last chance of safety, to take ship and flee beyond
the sea. The issue of events has often shown that it
is safer to rule over willing subjects than over such as
are disaffected. Nero found this out, Domitian too;
and in our own times Henry, duke of Saxony and

* Verg. Æn. iv. 569.

Bavaria.* Better it is for any prince to be more loved than feared by those who are set under him; it is expedient, however, that he be feared as well, provided that the fear proceed rather from good-will than from coercion.

Meanwhile Dermot, in the pursuit of Fortune that had fled from him, and strong in his hope for some happy turn of her wheel, ploughed through the sea with all sail set and with the winds blowing fair in answer to his prayers, and came to Henry II., king of the English, for the purpose of earnestly imploring aid. Although the king was in the far part of his realm, over sea, in Aquitanian Gaul, and much engaged in business, as kings are wont to be, yet he received him kindly and graciously enough, with that affability and courtesy which was inborn in him. Then on hearing the cause of his exile and the reason of his coming over, he accepted his bond of allegiance and oath of fealty, and granted him letters patent to the following effect:—" Henry, king of England, duke of Normandy and Aquitaine, and count of Anjou, to all his liegemen, English, Normans, Welsh and Scots, and to all nations subject to his sway sends greeting. Whensoever these our letters shall come unto you, know ye that we have taken Dermot, prince of the men of Leinster, into the bosom of our grace and goodwill. Wherefore, too, whosoever within the bounds of our dominions shall be willing to lend aid to him, as being

* Henry the Lion. He was deposed in 1180 by the emperor Frederic I. (Barbarossa), on a charge of having overstrained his power.

our vassal and liegeman, in the recovery of his own, let him know that he hath our favour and permission to that end."

A.D. 1166 or 1167.—Of the return of Dermot through Greater Britain.

Girald. Cambr. Expug. Hibern. Lib. I. cap. ii.

So Dermot, returning through Greater Britain, betook himself to the noble town of Bristol;* and honoured and loaded though he had been with many gifts by the royal munificence, yet he was buoyed up far more by hope than by any actual assistance he had yet obtained. There, spending his money right royally, he stayed for some time, on account of the frequent service of ships between that port and · Ireland: in this way he hoped to hear what was doing in his own realm and among his own people. While there he often had the royal letters read in public, and made liberal offers both of land and money to many persons, but without effect. At last Richard, earl of Strigul,† came to treat with him; when after a lengthy conference it was agreed that the earl on his part should in the coming spring assist him to regain his own, while Dermot pledged himself faithfully to give his eldest daughter to the

* Then the third city of England in importance: Norwich being the second and London the first. While at Bristol Dermot stayed in the house of one Robert Harding (Herdin) at St. Austins.

† See Note on him, Book I. chap. xii. of Gerald.

earl as wife, together with the succession to his kingdom.*

Matters being thus arranged, Dermot, drawn by that love for one's native soil which is natural to all, was fired with a yearning to see his fatherland, and without further delay went on to St. David's in South Wales. From here to Leinster over the intervening sea is but one day's sail; indeed, the opposite coasts are within sight of each other. Everybody knows that at that time Rhys ap Griffith was prince in those parts under the overlordship of the king, and that David, second of his name, was bishop of St. David's.† Each of them showed much kindly sympathy with the misfortunes of the exiled prince.

(Through the mediation of the bishop of St. David's, a contract was made with king Dermot, by which Robert Fitz-Stephen and Maurice Fitz-Gerald engaged to help him in the ensuing spring to recover his territories. Dermot, however, in his impatience crossed to Ireland at the first opportunity [*Aug.*, 1167], but passed the winter quietly at Ferns, then the capital of Leinster, where he found an asylum in the monastery. He seems to have taken with him as a protection one Richard Fitz-Godobert, a knight of Pembrokeshire, and a few English soldiers, "seventy heroes, dressed in coats of mail" [*Four Masters*]. But Roderic, the high-king, forced him to send his new allies back, after which he was apparently allowed to remain unmolested in his hereditary province of Kenceleia during the year 1168, his appeal for English aid having possibly frightened his enemies. Meanwhile he was waiting his time for revenge.)

---

* According to Brehon law Dermot had no right to make such an arrangement.

† This was David Fitz-Gerald, uncle of Gerald de Barri, and first *bishop* of St. David's (Menevia): his predecessors had been archbishops. Archbishop David I. was St. David, the first occupant of the see.

A.D. 1169.—The coming of Fitz-Stephen and the taking of Wexford.

Girald. Cambr. Expug. Hibern. Lib. I. cap. iii.

Meanwhile Robert Fitz-Stephen, mindful of his promise and true to his word,* had got together 30 men-at-arms of his own kinsmen and retainers, and also 60 others clad in mail, as well as 300 archers on foot,† the pick of Wales. Putting these on three ships, he sailed into the creek of Bannow ‡ about the first of May.

It is clear that then was the well-known prophecy of Merlin the Wild § fulfilled :—

> A knight of nature twain shall be the first,
> Hibernia's bonds by dint of arms to burst.

For if you wish to read aright this mystic saying of the seer, consider the ancestry of Fitz-Stephen on either side.‖

* But he was a year late.

† The Welsh longbow-men (the pattern of the famous English archers) were on foot, but there were also crossbow-men, who were sometimes mounted, sometimes not.

‡ About fifteen miles S. of Wexford, as the crow flies.

§ The three great Christian bards of mediæval Welsh legend were Merlin Ambrosius, Merlin Celidonius or Silvester ("the Wild"), and Merlin Taliessin. Of these the first and second were believed to possess the gifts of prophecy and enchantment. Ambrosius was generally referred to the times of Vortigern, and the reign of king Arthur. Silvester was supposed to have flourished in the sixth century.

‖ On his father's side he was Anglo-Norman, on his mother's side Welsh [*see Genealogical Table*]. His coat-of-arms, too, was party per pale.

14. THE LANDING OF FITZ-STEPHEN. 1169

With the same band there went over also Hervey de Montmaurice, a man of broken fortunes, without equipment or money; not so much to take part in the fighting as to act as a spy for earl Richard, whose uncle he was upon the father's side. Then landing on an island in the creek, they drew their vessels up along the shore and forthwith sent to Dermot news of their arrival. Naturally the fame of it soon spread abroad, and some of those who dwelt about the coast and had formerly left Dermot when his prospects changed for worse, at once came back to loyalty now that his luck had turned. For, as the poet says, 'tis ever so :—

With fortune stands or falls fidelity.*

(Dermot with 500 men joins the invaders, and all march to attack Wexford, which lay about twelve miles from the landing-place.)

When this was known, the townsmen, who hitherto had been invincible,† emboldened by their old success in arms marched out to the number of about 2000 men, and meeting the enemy while yet near his camp, stoutly drew up for fight. But when they saw lines arrayed in a strictness of order which was strange to them, and a troop of horse, splendid in hauberk, shield

---

* Ovid, 2 *Pont.* iii. 10.

† They were Ostmen [Norwegians], and superior in race, discipline and equipment to the native Irish. These Northmen, who were settled also at Waterford, Carlingford, Limerick, Dublin, Strangford, Wicklow, etc., were the only really formidable opponents with whom the invaders had to deal. Oxmantown is the town of the Ostmen, or Eastmen.

and gleaming helm, as circumstances had changed, they changed their plans, and after firing the suburbs straightway retired within the ramparts. Fitz-Stephen and his followers on their part eagerly prepared for the assault: the men in mail lined the ditches, the archers were posted in the rear to command the advanced towers, and then, loudly cheering, all rushed forward with one heart to attack the walls. But the townsmen, ready of defence, proceeded to hurl from the battlements great beams and stones, and repulsed the besiegers with considerable loss. Among the wounded was one Robert de Barri,* who 'with the ardour of youthful valour despised in his eagerness the risk of death. As he led the way among those who were first scaling the fortifications, he was struck upon the helmet by a stone, and falling headlong down into the bottom of the ditch, was with great difficulty dragged out alive by his comrades. (Owing to the force of the stroke, sixteen years afterwards his double teeth fell out; and, what is still more astonishing, new ones at once grew in their places.) Drawing off, therefore, from the walls they hastened to the neighbouring shore, and set fire to all the ships they found lying on the strand. . . . On the morrow, however, after high mass had been solemnized in full parade, they advanced to the assault; this time with greater caution, and their array more carefully disposed. But when, in firm reliance no less on the resources of skill than on their bravery, in other words trusting as much in their warlike arts as in their valiant

* Elder brother of Gerald de Barri.

hearts, the besiegers drew near the walls, the townsmen abandoned all hope of defending them, and reflecting that they were wrong in resisting their lawful prince, set themselves rather to offer terms. Through the mediation, therefore, of the bishops, for two of them at that juncture were in the town, and of other worthy and well-disposed men, peace was re-established, and the townsmen submitted to Dermot, handing over four hostages for their fidelity in the time to come. He, the more to animate his allies, and being desirous of at once rewarding the leaders for their first success, then and there assigned the town with all its dependent territory to Fitz-Stephen and Maurice; and this was due to them in accordance with the original agreement. To Hervey de Montmaurice, too, he gave to hold in fee two hundreds [*cantreds*] situate between the towns, Wexford that is and Waterford, and bordering on the sea.*

A.D. 1169.—Of the conquest of the men of Ossory.

Girald. Cambr. Expug. Hibern. Lib. 1. cap. iv.

This enterprise having been completed with all the success they could desire, they joined to their own forces the men of Wexford, and with an army about 3000 strong directed their march on Ossory. Now amongst all the rebellious vassals of Dermot ever most hostile to him had been Donnell, lord of Ossory; and some time before, when he held in captivity Dermot's

---

* These grants were all in fee, and here again Dermot was acting without regard to the laws of his country.

son, stung by jealousy he had carried his vengeance to such a pitch as to put out his eyes. At first the invaders did not penetrate far into the district of Ossory, for almost on the very borders they found the inhabitants posted in a region fenced in with woods and impassable for swamps; and they proved no weaklings in defending their fatherland. Nay, rendered confident by the success of their defence, they even pursued their enemies right away to the open plains. But there the knights of Fitz-Stephen turned, and charging fiercely wrought no little slaughter among them, spearing them as they scattered in flight over the level country and dispersing them in utter rout; while those whom the horsemen had dashed to the ground, were quickly decapitated by the broad axes * of the Irish foot. Thus, then, was the victory gained, and some 200 of his enemies' heads were laid at the feet of Dermot. To see whose they were he turned them over one by one; then thrice did he clap his hands and leap for joy, and giving thanks to the Most High burst into exultant song. Ay, and even the head of one whom he had hated above the rest he took up by the ears and hair and in a most blood-

---

* The "sparthe," or iron battle-axe, the use of which the Irish had learnt from the Ostmen [Girald. *Top*. Dis. iii. c. 10 below]. These 500 men whom Dermot had contributed to the expedition were probably "gallowglasses," infantry equipped and armed after the Norwegian fashion [*Expug*. i. 21]. They formed the body-guard, "hus-carls" as it were, of the native chieftains, and were regular soldiers, quite distinct from the kernes, or light-armed militia-men, who constituted the bulk of an Irish army.

B

thirsty and brutal manner tore away with his teeth the lips and nose.

(Gerald has apparently run two battles into one, as the following extracts from Regan and from Carew's Abstract of Regan will show. The actual events were: 1. The English forced the entrenchments of the men of Ossory, and put the latter to flight, as told in the subjoined portion of the poem. 2. The conquerors then set to plundering and devastating the country, after which they started to retire with their spoil into Kinselagh [*Kenceleia*]. 3. Meanwhile the Ossorians had rallied under cover of the woods, and occupied a defile through which the retreating Anglo-Irish force would have to pass. An engagement ensued which is described in the first passage from Carew below.)

A.D. 1169.—[Another account of the conquest of Ossory.]

Regan's Anglo-Norman Poem, ll. 524-617.

(Before starting for Ossory Dermot calls a council of his English allies.)

> Now when to Dermot's royal hall
>   The barons bold were come,
> He straight unfolded his design,
>   And counsel asked of some.
> He told how rebel Ossorie,
>   From churl to faithless lord,
> Unnerved by sense of perjured troth,
>   Quaked at the English sword.
> 'Wherefore, sirs barons,' quoth the king,
>   'Since thus they dread our might,
> To Ossorie I fain would go
>   These guilty foes to smite.'

Then out the barons answered him,
    Upstanding there around,
That never would they toil eschew,
Nor cease such vassals false to sue,
    Or ever they be found.
And ere the line of march was formed,
    The bruit of English aid
Brought in three thousand Irish foot *
    To swell the king's brigade.
But when the barons saw the power,
    That flocked from all the coast,
With heightened cheer and heartsome trust
    They joined the mingled host.

*   *   *   *   *

Athwart their path the foemen lay,
    A full five thousand strong,
The which the lord of Ossorie
    Had marshalled in his throng;
Mac Donnell e'en, the traitor prince
    Of caitiff Ossorie,
Who there had built himself a hold
    Made stout with dike and tree.
For, deft of spade, his knaves had drawn
    Three fosses broad and deep
A pace apart; in rear of all
    A stockade crowned the steep.
And there the felon battle gave
    To king Dermot next day;
From sunrise unto eventide
    Each side bore up the fray.

    * Some of these were Ostmen of Wexford.

Then furious swayed the tide of war,
  Then strove despair with zeal,
Till ousted were the rebel horde
  By English thews and steel.
But many a wound was ta'en and dealt,
  And many a life fordone;
And stark lay knight and gallowglass,
Archer and kerne, in motley mass,
  Before the post was won.
Right proud and joyous was the king
  Such feat of arms to see;
How fame and vengeance both were his
  By force of Englishrie.
At morn, in strength of victory,
  He gave the land to flame,
Forwasted all, or far or near,
  To cleanse away its shame.
From here, from there, from cot and thorpe,
  Was prize and trophy reft;
O'er hill and plain, in wood and dale,
  Till naught to spoil was left.

A.D. 1169.—[Another account of the conquest of Ossory, *continued.*]

Regan's Anglo-Norman Poem: Carew's Prose Abstract.

(The Irish had occupied a pass which lay in the English line of retreat.)

" According to his [*Dermot's*] direction the English prepared themselves to fight. The king [*Dermot*] for his safety put himself into their battalion; his son, Donnell Kavenagh, he commanded with 43 Kenceleia men to be in the forlorn hope. The rest of his forces, which were 1700, mingled not with the English, for they [*the latter*] mistrusted such as could run like the wind.

Donnell Kavenagh was no sooner entered the pass, but the enemy assailed him, and he was enforced to shelter himself under the English. After the fight had continued three hours, prince Donnell's [*lord of Ossory*] men began to faint, gave ground, and ran away; nevertheless in an instant they rallied again, and made a new head. In the interim the English horse and foot were gotten into a low moorish ground, wherein Donnell [*lord of Ossory*] assured himself to have a fair day upon them. Maurice de Prendergast, apprehending the danger they were in, with a loud voice called upon his companions:—'Let us,' said he, 'withstand our enemies, and free ourselves out of this bottom. We are well armed and they are naked; if we may recover hard ground we shall be freed from peril, and there is no doubt but they be ours, or at the least we shall die with honour.' Then he called upon one named Robert Smith:—'Take,' said he, '50 soldiers, and lie in ambush in yonder thicket, and move not until the Irish be past. If they will charge you, we will come to your succour;' which direction was immediately obeyed. Donnell [*lord of Ossory*] and his men, which were about 2000, conceiving that the English began to faint, came boldly on, passed the ambush (which, being so few, durst not stir), and gave a furious charge. Dermot, then fearing that all was lost, prayed Maurice [*de Prendergast*] to have care to succour those which were left in ambush. 'Be not dismayed,' said Maurice, 'when it shall be needful I will have care to relieve them.' The Irish with great eagerness continued the skirmish, and continually charged them upon their retreat, until they had recovered hard ground. Then Maurice de Prendergast, Robert Fitz-Stephen, Meiler Fitz-Henry, Milo Fitz-David [*i.e. Milo Fitz-Gerald*], Hervey de Montmaurice, with other English knights, turned upon the men of Ossory and in a moment they [*the latter*] were discomfited. All of them [*the English*] did admirably well; but Meiler Fitz-Henry deserved the most honour. When the Irish that were with Dermot, who all the time of the fight for fear had hidden themselves in the wood, saw the enemy broken, they followed the chase and fell to the execution of Donnell's [*lord of Ossory*] men. Two hundred and twenty were slain, whose heads were presented to Dermot; and many also afterwards died of their hurts."

(Some time after this Donnell, lord of Ossory, tendered his submission, although he had no intention of abiding by it.)

A.D. 1169.—[Defection of Maurice de Prendergast.]

Regan's Anglo-Norman Poem: Carew's Prose Abstract.

"Dermot being grown proud with his victories gave discontentment to the English; insomuch as Maurice de Prendergast with 200 soldiers went to Wexford, with a resolution there to embark and pass into Wales. Whereof when Dermot had knowledge, he sent to Wexford requiring the townsmen to give impediment. Maurice, seeing his passage stopped, and offended with Dermot, by the advice of the Wexford men, who hated the king, sent to Donnell, king of Ossory, proposing to serve him against Dermot; who joyfully accepted of the proffer and promised him great entertainment. Maurice, in his march towards Tech-Moylin [*Timoling or St. Mullins, co. Carlow*], was forlaid and encountered by Donnell Kavenagh, king Dermot's son, with 500 foot. But Maurice forced his way, and came safely to Tech-Moylin, where he remained three days; and there the king of Ossory came to him, well and strongly attended. The conditions on either part being agreed upon, and Donnell and Maurice sworn each to the other for the true performing of them, they marched unto Ossory, whence, by the aid of Maurice, Donnell made incursions upon Dermot and spoiled his country. This departure of Maurice de Prendergast did not work the like effect in the rest; for Robert Fitz-Stephen, Hervey de Montmaurice, and other English knights, remained with the king of Leinster."

(Later on in the same year Prendergast, finding his position of hostility to his fellow-countrymen distasteful and his new Irish allies untrustworthy, returned to Wales with his men; but we soon find him back again in Ireland and taking part in the conquest once more.)

A.D. 1169.—League of all Ireland against Dermot and Fitz-Stephen.

Girald. Cambr. Expug. Hib. Lib. I. cap. v.

Meanwhile rolls on the wheel of fate : now fortune frowns, and threatens abasement to the exalted, ruin to the prosperous. For when the late successes of Dermot and the coming, too, of the dread foreigner, are noised abroad throughout the island, Roderic, prince of the men of Connaught and high-king of all Ireland, reflecting how from small beginnings great issues often spring, and being of a foreboding turn of mind, already foresaw the evils that menaced as much himself as the whole land from the invasion of the strangers. He therefore sent messengers to all the country round, and hastily convoked an assembly of the chief men of the island. After taking counsel together, forthwith the wrath of one and all was roused against Dermot, and they brought together into that part of Leinster which is called Kinselagh [*Kenceleia*] a great number of trained troops * and a vast multitude of kernes.†

* "Gallowglasses:" see Gerald. I. iv. above. They were divided into "battles," or companies, of from sixty to eighty men.

† Light infantry, without body-armour, but with the sides of the head and neck protected by their long hair plaited into "glibs." They carried either wicker shields or small bucklers of iron ; pikes or pairs of darts ; slings ; small iron-headed axes ; and "skenes" (dirks, about fifteen inches long, for stabbing, like the Roman short sword). These weapons were often of weak metal which bent at the blow, as we read that the long swords of the early Teutonic invaders of the Roman Empire

And now to Dermot. Some of his fair-weather friends, flitting like the swallow at the wintry blast, stole secretly away and vanished; others, holding light their oath of fealty, openly deserted to the foe. Thus in the hour of greatest need very few of his followers, besides Fitz-Stephen and his men, did he find true to him. He thereupon retired with those who still were faithful to a position not far from Ferns, which surrounded as it was by steep and densely wooded cliffs, by water and by marsh, afforded a natural vantage-ground that was entirely inaccessible. Here, under the directions of Fitz-Stephen, the soldiers began at once to fell the trees, to strengthen the underwood by interweaving boughs, to break up the surface of the ground by digging deep pits and ditches, and to clear secret and narrow passages of a tortuous nature in which they might entangle an attacking force, or by which they might themselves escape. In short, they made the place easy of ingress and egress for their own side, impassable for an enemy: and a position which was naturally difficult of assault, they fortified with the greatest industry and skill.

did. An engagement was generally begun by the kernes, who cast their javelins and so opened the way for the heavy axe-men to come to the hand-stroke; which reminds us how the archers in the English contingent under lord Rivers during the reconquest of Granada by Ferdinand and Isabella opened up gaps in the Moorish ranks wherein the battle-axe might do its work. Welsh and Irish kernes were afterwards used in the French wars to mingle in the *mêlée* and stab the horses of the French knights. The Scotch had their kernes and gallowglasses too (see Shak. *Macb.* I. 2).

A description of Dermot.

Girald. Cambr. Expug. Hibern. Lib. I. cap. vi.

Now Dermot was a man tall of stature and stout of frame: a soldier whose heart was in the fray, and held valiant among his own nation. From often shouting his battle-cry, his voice had become hoarse. A man who liked better to be feared by all than loved by any. One who would oppress his greater vassals, while he raised to high station men of lowly birth. A tyrant to his own subjects, he was hated by strangers: his hand was against every man, and every man's hand against him.

[The History resumed.]

Meanwhile Roderic sent to Fitz-Stephen messengers who proffered and promised gifts of great value, and used every argument to induce him to depart in peace and amity from a land, for his presence in which he could offer no sort of justification: yet was he not persuaded. Then the messengers appealed to Dermot to join his arms with theirs for the extermination of the foreigner, promising the peaceful restoration to him of all Leinster, together with the firm friendship of Roderic. Many arguments, too, did they adduce on behalf of their common fatherland; spending much entreaty and discourse in support of this. But their prayers availed them naught.

A.D. 1169.—How peace was re-established.

Girald. Cambr. Expug. Hibern. Lib. I. cap. x.

Roderic, knowing that the issues of war are ever doubtful, and that as the comic poet says,

'All ways will a wise man try before he takes to arms,' *

and also because he shrank from joining battle with knights in full armour as these strangers were, sent envoys to try by any means to get terms. And so, through the mediation of worthy men and by the favour of Heaven, peace was at length made upon the following conditions :—that Leinster should be left to Dermot, but that he should acknowledge Roderic as chief prince and high-king of Ireland, and yield him the submission thereby due. To secure this compact Dermot also gave his son Conor as a hostage; while Roderic pledged his word that if as time went on Dermot by his actions contributed to strengthen their concord, he would give his daughter in marriage to the young prince.

These stipulations were publicly announced, and oaths in confirmation of them mutually given and taken ; but in addition it was secretly agreed that for the future Dermot should invite no foreigners into the island, and moreover that those whom he had already called in should be sent back as soon as order had been restored in Leinster.

* Ter. *Eun.* 4. 7. 19. The quotation in the Latin text is not verbatim.

A.D. 1169.—The coming of Maurice [Fitz-Gerald] and the reduction of Dublin.

Girald. Cambr. Expug. Hibern. Lib. I. cap. xi.

The business being thus settled, fortune seemed to smile again and turn a serene countenance on Dermot's cause; for, lo! there put in to Wexford with two ships Maurice Fitz-Gerald of whom we spoke above, the uterine brother of Fitz-Stephen, accompanied by 10 men-at-arms, 30 mounted retainers, and about 100 archers on foot. Maurice was a discreet and honourable man; well known for his good faith, and of tried energy. Though of a modesty that was almost maidenly, yet he was famed for his stability of character. A gentleman; whose word was his bond.

Dermot was greatly delighted by this lucky arrival, which re-kindled his anxiety to avenge upon the men of Dublin the grave injuries they had so frequently offered to himself and to his father. He therefore lost no time in assembling the army and in preparing to march on that city. Meanwhile Fitz-Stephen was building a stronghold on a certain steep and rocky eminence, known among the natives as the 'Crag,' about two furlongs from Wexford: a natural fortification, the strength of which was now increased by art. Maurice, however, was associated with Dermot in the command of the English forces in the field, and acted as leader of the campaign. In a short space of time all the domain of the city together with the adjacent provinces was reduced almost to desolation by plunder, fire and sword. At length the citizens sued for peace, and gave good security for their future loyalty to their king and for yielding the obedience that was due to him.

While this was going on hostilities had broken out between Roderic of Connaught and Donnell [O'Brien, king] of Limerick, and directly Roderic with an armed force crossed the borders of Limerick, Dermot despatched Fitz-Stephen and his men to the aid of Donnell, who was his son-in-law. With the support of this reinforcement, O'Brien, after several engagements, in all of which he was successful, drove Roderic back with shame and disgrace into his own territories and entirely freed himself from his supremacy.

A.D. 1169. —Of the preparations of earl Richard.

Girald. Cambr. Expug. Hibern. Lib. I. cap. xii.

Dermot had now recovered all his hereditary possessions, and began to look for higher things. He aspired to the ancient ancestral position of his house, and meditated the subjection of Connaught by force of arms, and the gaining of the high-kingship of Ireland for himself. With a view, therefore, to this he had a secret conference with Fitz-Stephen and Maurice, and made a full revelation to them of his design. They answered that it could easily be realized if he were to procure the assistance of more English troops. On this, after using every entreaty to induce them to invite into the island their kinsmen and countrymen in greater numbers and to take in hand

30 DERMOT'S LETTER TO STRONGBOW 1169

the accomplishment of his project, at length, the more effectually to persuade them to it, he offered to either of them his eldest daughter in marriage together with the succession to the kingdom. But as at the time each rejoiced in the possession of a lawful wife, after much deliberation he finally settled on the plan of sending messengers with the following letter to earl Richard, whom we have mentioned above, and to whom formerly when in Bristol he had promised to give this same daughter to wife.

'Dermot Mac Murrough, king of Leinster, to Richard, earl of Strigul, son of earl Gilbert, greeting.

Were you, like us who lack your aid, to count the lingering days,
That samely pass and pass again before you glad our gaze,
You would allow not overtimely chide we these delays.*

We have watched the storks and swallows: the summer birds have come; come, ay, and flown again before the ocean blast. Neither eastern breeze nor zephyr's breath wafts to us your longed-for, looked-for presence. Let the prompt fulfilment of your promise cure this malady of delay; let your deeds show that "your tryst is but deferred, not broken." † All Leinster now is ours again. If you are timely with us, and in force, the other four divisions can easily be added to the fifth. Wherefore right grateful will you render your arrival, if it be speedy; glorious will it be, if soon; the earlier the more welcome. Renewed affection heals the wounds

* Adapted from Ovid. *Ep. Her.* ii. 7.
† Ovid. *Ep. Her.* ii. 102.

of love, provided only those wounds be dealt in part by neglect. For friendship is restored by kindly offices, and grows by services to greater strength.'

After perusing this letter, earl Richard carefully turned the matter over in his mind and at last came to a decision as to his course of action; a decision based on the luck that had attended his fellow-countrymen. For taking heart from the success of Fitz-Stephen, which he had before considered doubtful, he directed his best energies to the Irish expedition, fixed all his aspirations on it, and in every way roused himself to the conquest of the island.

The earl * was of high descent, for he was born of the noble stock of the house of Clare. Yet withal, so far, a man whose family was better than his fortune; who had more blue blood than brains, and whose pedigree was longer than his purse. He went, then, to Henry II., king of the English, and earnestly begged and entreated him either as a mere act of

* Richard Fitz-Gilbert de Clare, 2nd earl of Pembroke, called also earl of Striguil, or Estrigoil, from one of his castles about four miles from Chepstow. He was called Strongbow, apparently by the Flemings and English in his service in S. Wales, a nickname borne first by his father Gilbert. He succeeded to his earldom in 1149, but was in disgrace with the king, who had deprived him of his estate. The proposals of Dermot seemed to offer a prospect of repairing his fortunes. In spite of Gerald's description of him [chap. xxvii. below] he was undoubtedly a captain of considerable repute; at any rate sufficiently so to render Henry extremely uneasy with regard to the position he made for himself in Ireland. His arms were Or, three chevrons, gules [*Clare*], a label of five points, azure [*personal*].

justice to restore to him the domains which were his by hereditary right, or to grant him leave to try his fate and lot in foreign lands.

A.D. 1170.—The coming of Reimund [Fitz-Gerald] and the defeat of the men of Waterford at Dundunnolf.

Girald. Cambr. Expug. Hibern. Lib. 1. cap. xiii.

On receiving a kind of permission from the king, though it was given in jest rather than in earnest,* when the winter was over he sent on before him into Ireland about the 1st of May [?] a young knight of his household, Reimund by name, with 10 men-at-arms and 70 archers. He was powerful and robust of body, and trained to arms; a nephew of both Fitz-Stephen and Maurice, for he was a son of their elder brother. Landing at a rocky headland called Dundunnolf, about four miles from Waterford and south of Wexford, they threw up a slight entrenchment of boughs and sods. But the citizens of Waterford and Melaghlin O'Phelan, lord of Decies,†—for report of the landing soon spread abroad—looked with suspicion on the vicinity of the foreigners, and after conferring together determined to meet the evil at the outset and to take up arms in common against the invader. So, to the number of about 3000 men, they crossed the river Suir, which flows close under the

* Later on the king absolutely prohibited the enterprise, but this was disregarded by the earl.

† A considerable district in what was afterwards the county of Waterford. The latter is not mentioned as a shire till 1251.

walls on the eastern side of the city and divides Desmond from Leinster. Then, forming in three divisions for the assault, they marched bravely up to the entrenchments. . . . Reimund and his garrison, few as they were in number, yet with remarkable gallantry sallied out to meet them, and joined battle against great odds. But as such a handful of men, however valiant, clearly could not hold their own against so vast a multitude, they fell back on the camp, and the foremost of the enemy, who were pressing on their rear, got into the entrance in the confusion and prevented the gates from being shut. Then Reimund seeing that he and his followers were in a strait, nay, in imminent jeopardy of their lives, like a brave man turned his face to the foe and cut down in the gateway with his good sword the first of the pursuers who crossed the threshold. The noble stand he made, that single blow, and the ring of his battle-cry, both rallied his own men to the defence and struck terror into the enemy. Thus then—for the fortune of war, as it were, hangs ever on the cast of a die—those who had seemed conquered, in a moment became the victors, and scattering their opponents in flight over the plain pursued them with such carnage that 500 and more were speedily killed. And when the pursuers ceased from sheer fatigue to use their swords, they flung great numbers of the fugitives from the lofty cliffs into the sea. . . . On that field the pride of Waterford was humbled: on that field her power was broken. That victory began the overthrow of a noble city, and while it brought hope and encouragement to the English, to the natives it brought horror and despair. For it was a thing unheard of in those parts that so small a band should have wrought so great a slaughter.*

A.D. 1170.—The coming of the earl and the taking of Waterford.

Girald. Cambr. Expug. Hibern. Lib. I. cap. xvi.

In the meantime earl Richard, having finished the preparations for his great enterprise, marched for St. David's along the coast-road of South Wales,† enlisting as he went picked men out of those parts. When all that was necessary for so important a voyage had been procured or completed, he embarked at Milford Haven with 200 men-at-arms and about 1000 others.‡ The wind blew fair from the east, and he made land

---

* These conflicts of small numbers of well-armed and highly trained men with large ill-ordered hosts resemble the battles of Cortez and Pizarro in Mexico and Peru respectively, and of Clive in India.

† Probably the old Roman road. The earl's route, then, would be from his chief castle of Chepstow through Caerleon, Neath, Llwchwr, and Carmarthen to St. David's, and his recruits would therefore be drawn from what are now the counties of Monmouth, Glamorgan, Carmarthen, and Pembroke. But the shires of Monmouth and Carmarthen had not been formed at that time. Between Neath and Llwchwr, and again soon after entering Pembroke, he would leave on his left the Flemish colonies established by Henry I. in Gowerland and Haverfordwest respectively. He may have enlisted men from these.

‡ Archers.

near Waterford a little before the beginning of September: the exact day being the eve of St. Bartholomew [23d *August*].

Then was fulfilled the prophecy of Merlin the Wild :—

> First flares the flaming torch,
> Then blazes up the fire;
> As the spark lit up the torch,
> Kindles that torch our pyre.*

So too the saying of Moling the Erseman :—' A great man will come, forerunner of a greater, who shall set his heel on Desmond's neck and bruise the head of Leinster; and by force of arms shall go with glory on the way prepared before him.'

Next day, on hearing of the landing of the earl, Reimund was filled with joy, and attended by 40 men-at-arms hastened to meet him. The former had already set up his standard before the city, and on the morning of the feast,† being the day of the war-god,‡ the united forces marched with banners displayed to the attack. But after the burghers, aided

---

* The spark represents the landing of Fitz-Stephen (chap. iii. of Gerald, above), the torch the coming of the earl, while the final invasion by Henry III. in person is to complete the cremation of Ireland's freedom. The "great man" in Moling's prediction is the earl, the "greater" of course Henry II. St. Moling was archbishop of Ferns, 632–696, in the time of the supremacy of Northumbria in England. The day of his death and his saint's day was June 17.

† Of St. Bartholomew; see above.

‡ "Dies Martis" in the text: that is Tuesday, the day of Tiw, the god of war.

by those who had escaped from the carnage at Dundunnolf, had twice manfully repulsed them, Reimund, who now by common consent had been made commander-in-chief of the whole army and in whose hands had been placed the conduct of the campaign, noticed a kind of shed fixed to the outside of the wall, and supported by posts. He at once called together his men in full force for an assault, and quickly sent forward some of the mail-clad soldiers to cut away the posts. This done, the shed fell in a heap, dragging with it a considerable portion of the wall. Through the breach thus made the besiegers poured eagerly into the city, butchered whole crowds of the citizens in the streets, and gained a most bloody victory. In Reginald's Tower * the two Sihtrics were taken and put to the sword. In like manner Reginald himself and Melaghlin O'Phelan † were captured in the same place, but through the intervention of Dermot, who came up just then with Maurice and Fitz-Stephen, their lives were spared. A garrison was placed in the city, and the daughter of Dermot, Eva by name,‡ was there given away by her father in lawful wedlock to the earl, and the alliance cemented by the marriage. Then all started to march on Dublin.

* Now the Ring Tower. A round keep built by the Ostmen at an angle of the city walls. Reginald was the "king" of the Norse colony in Waterford. The two Sihtrics appear to have been Norse chiefs under him. Doubtless they all made their last stand in this tower.

† Chap. xiii. of Gerald above.

‡ This was the lady mentioned above (Bk. I. chaps. xii. and ii. of Gerald above).

A.D. 1170.—Of the storming of the city of Dublin.

Girald. Cambr. Expug. Hibern. Lib. I. cap. xvii.

Dermot, however, knowing that almost all Ireland had been summoned by the citizens of Dublin to aid in the defence,* and that every road leading to the city ran through wooded defiles held by the enemy, remembered the disaster † that befel his father, and avoiding the forest country led his army along the mountain ridges ‡ by Glendalough,§ and brought it safely to the city walls. For he held the inhabitants of Dublin in deeper detestation than any other of his enemies in Ireland; and not without reason, since they had murdered his father in the great hall of one of his chief men where he was accustomed to sit in public to administer justice, and had added insult to injury by burying a dog with the body. Envoys, however, were sent from the city, and preliminaries of peace were entered into through the special mediation of Laurence, of blessed memory, then archbishop of the see of Dublin.‖ But in the mean time on one side of the city Reginald, on the other a certain Milo de Cogan, a valiant officer, with a following of the younger soldiery thirsting for fight and plunder, carried the walls with a rush and descended boldly into the city, making much slaughter among the

* 30,000 men had come, under Roderic of Connaught.
† Clearly a defeat, though the time and details seem unknown.
‡ Like Fabius in the Hannibalian War.
§ "The dale of the two lakes," in Wicklow, about twenty-two miles south of Dublin.
‖ Of him below, Gerald, Bk. II. chap. xxiv.

people.* The greater number of these, however, led by Hasculf, got on board their galleys and boats with their more valuable effects and sailed off to the Northern Islands.† On the same day two great miracles happened in the city. A crucifix which the citizens tried hard to carry away with them to the isles became immovable; and a penny which was twice offered before the same, twice leapt back.

(Milo de Cogan is left by the earl as governor of Dublin. Roderic of Connaught, in retaliation for an irruption by Dermot and his allies beyond the borders of Leinster into the territory of his old enemy O'Ruarc, king of Meath, after in vain warning Dermot, put to death the son of the latter whom he held as a hostage [chap. x. of Gerald above].)

A.D. 1170.—The council at Armagh.

Girald. Cambr. Expug. Hibern. Lib. I. cap. xviii.

After these events a general assembly of the Irish clergy was held at Armagh, and the coming of the strangers into Ireland was discussed at some length. Finally they arrived at the following conclusion :—That it must be for the sins of their countrymen, and especially in punishment for their inveterate custom of indiscriminately buying Englishmen from merchants, bandits, and pirates, and using them as slaves, that

* This act of treachery on the part of the English is spoken of in the Four Masters as "a miracle wrought against them [*the Ostmen*] ... in consequence of their violation of their word to the men of Ireland."

† The isles to the west and north of Scotland were settled by their Norwegian fellow-countrymen, as also was Man.

the vengeance of Heaven had inflicted this evil upon them, whereby they themselves by a just retaliation were in turn reduced to servitude by that very nation. For it had been the vicious but common practice of the English people, when their kingdom was yet intact,* to offer the children of their country for sale, and that too without the excuse of poverty or famine; indeed, they would send their own sons and kinsmen to Ireland to be sold. Whence it can readily be believed that for the perpetration of such an enormity the buyers had now deserved the yoke of slavery, even as the sellers had had to undergo it in former times.† Wherefore it was decreed by the aforesaid council and by general assent publicly proclaimed that throughout the island all Englishmen who were held in bondage should be restored to liberty.

A.D. 1170.—[Convocation of the clergy at Clonfert.]
Annals of Clonmacnoise; 1170: *Mageoghegan's MS. Translation from the Irish.*

"In the year one thousand one hundred and seventy last mentioned there was a great convocation of the clergy of Ireland at Clonfert by commission from the pope [*Alexander III.*] for the reformation

---

* *i.e.* before the Norman Conquest. After the conquest the slave-trade was prohibited by William I., Wulfstan, bishop of Worcester, being the Wilberforce of the time. But it still went on, especially at Bristol, and the decision of the Council of Armagh seems to have been intended to prevent Henry from urging this as a pretext for the invasion, though we do not find it mentioned as a reason in his appeal to the pope to sanction the enterprise.   † Alluding to the Norman Conquest.

of certain abuses of a long time used in Ireland. . . .
There it was laid down by them by constitution that
no layman should have the rule of any church or
church matters from henceforth. . . . That holy
orders should be given to bishops' or priests' sons.
And for example of these their constitutions they took
the livings of seven bishops that had bishopricks and
were laymen."

(The success of the invasion had by this time turned
Henry II.'s contempt for it into jealousy, for to permit anything like an "imperium in imperio" had been directly contrary
to Crown policy since the Norman Conquest. He now [1170]
issued an edict recalling the adventurers and placing the Irish
ports under a kind of "nominal blockade," and so cut off the
English forces in the island from their supplies. The earl,
being therefore in great distress, sent off Reimund to the court
in Aquitaine to say that he placed his Irish conquests un-
reservedly at the royal disposal. The messenger could get no
reply. Hervey de Montmaurice was then despatched to regain
the king's favour.)

Radulph. Nig. Contin. 1170.

[Henry] had in mind to appoint him [*i.e. his son
John, then a child*] king of Ireland, for he had taken
that island away from his loyal subject Richard, earl
of Strigul, who had lawfully acquired it by his own
valour, and held it as the heritage of his wife.

[**May 1st, A.D. 1171.—Death of Dermot, king of
Leinster.**]

Annals of the Four Masters: 1171; *O'Donovan's
Translation from the Irish.*

"Dermot Mac Murrough, king of Leinster, by
whom a trembling sod was made of all Ireland—after

having brought over the Saxons, after having done extensive injuries to the Irish, after plundering and burning many churches . . .—died before the end of a year (after this plundering), of an insufferable and unknown disease. For he became putrid while living, through the miracle of God, Colum-cille, and Finnan,* and other saints of Ireland, whose churches he had profaned and burned some time before; and he died at Fearna-mor [*Ferns*] without (making) a will, without penance, without the body of Christ, without unction, as his evil deeds deserved."

May 16th, A.D. 1171.—Overthrow of the Ostmen at Dublin.

Girald. Cambr. Expug. Hibern. Lib. 1. cap. xxi.

About the same time, on White-Sunday [*May 16th*], Hasculf, formerly king of the [Ost]men of Dublin, burning for revenge, sailed into the Liffey with Norwegians and islanders in 60 galleys to attack the city. They poured from the vessels in eager haste, led by John surnamed the 'Wood'—'Insanus' or 'Vehemens' in the Latin tongue—, a man of warlike soul. All, in Danish fashion, were clad in mail; some in ring hauberks reaching low, others in tegulated armour † of skilful make. Their shields were round and painted

---

* Abbot of Clonard in Meath. Said to have been the tutor of upwards of 3000 Irish saints. He died in 548, and his saint's day is December 12th.

† Small tile-shaped plates sewn on to a leather jerkin. The plates were sometimes made of bone, but not so here, as the Latin text expressly states.

red,* and iron-bound about the rim. They were men of iron hearts as well as iron arms. In ordered array they advanced to the walls hard by the eastern gate [*St. Mary's Port*].

But Milo de Cogan, who was then governor of the city, though the garrison was far inferior in numbers, with all the intrepidity of his nature boldly sallied out to meet them. With so small a band, however, he could not stand against the onset of the enemy, and after losing some of his men—one of whom had his thigh, though it was encased in steel, together with the skirt of his mail-shirt cut through with one blow of an axe †—, he was pressed back and compelled to retire within the gate; when Richard de Cogan, Milo's brother, who had quietly issued with a few followers from the southern postern, fell with fierce shouts upon the rear of the Ostmen. Owing to this unlooked-for and sudden event, and attacked as they were on front and flank, the enemy were soon beaten, and took to flight. So doubtful ever are the chances of war. Almost all were put to the sword, including John the Wood: the latter, indeed, defended himself right well, but was at length taken and killed by Walter de Ridenesford aided by some others. Hasculf was haled back from the sea-shore, over which he was fleeing to his galleys, and to grace the victory was led alive into the city where he had so lately ruled. It

---

* Red was the national colour of the Scandinavian races, and may survive in the red coats of our soldiers to this day.

† This feat was performed by John the Wood, who slew also nine or ten other Englishmen [*Regan*].

was intended to keep him for ransom, and he was brought before Milo in the justice-hall, when in his wrath he burst out in the presence of everybody with this imprudent speech :—' We came with a mere handful of men this time ; * it was but a first attempt. But only let me live, and you shall see a very different effort, one to which this will be a trifle.' On hearing this, Milo had him at once beheaded.

* * * * *

(Owing to Henry II.'s prohibition of intercourse with Ireland, the English there were reduced to great straits for want of food and reinforcements. Encouraged by this archbishop Laurence and Roderic of Connaught roused the native princes to besiege the earl in Dublin, and invited Guthred, king of Man, and the Norse wickings of the isles to co-operate by sea. The latter were ready enough to do so, apart from the promised pay, for they felt anxious at the progress of the English arms in Ireland. When the siege had lasted nearly two months, the defenders, who were almost starved out, made, by the advice of Maurice Fitz-Gerald and Milo de Cogan, a desperate sortie, in which they routed and dispersed the besiegers, although the latter are said to have numbered 60,000 men. The garrison then marched to the relief of the camp at the "Crag," where Fitz-Stephen had for some time been beleaguered by the men of Wexford and Kinselagh [*Kenceleia*], who were in revolt. While on the way, the earl heard that Fitz-Stephen and his little band had been taken by treachery and their stake and turf-built fort destroyed [1171].)

---

* The numbers are given by Regan as high as 20,000, in 100 galleys. It was like a Northman to break out in this reckless way, though he might well be wroth, not only at the beating he had just received, but also at the recollection of the treachery of the English by which he originally lost Dublin (chap. xvii. of Gerald above).

44 FITZ-MAURICE ADVISES A SALLY. 1171

A.D. 1171.—The speech of [Fitz-]Maurice [advising the sally from Dublin].
Girald. Cambr. Expug. Hibern. Lib. I. cap. xxiii.

' 'Tis not in search of pleasure, men, nor as summoned to a life of ease, that we are in this land. Rather 'tis to challenge the ups and downs of destiny, and at the peril of our lives to test the mettle of our manhood. At times whirled aloft to Fortune's highest pitch, to-day, see, we are precipitated to her lowest depths! Such the rotations of her flying wheel! Such the mutability of mundane things! Thus in checkered change do good and ill hap alternate. The sun goes up the sky, the heavens revolve, and even so it sets again. Eastward it wends its way, and the beams of its rise in turn light up once more the shadows of the West. We whom hitherto a glorious and triumphant prosperity has provided with all that we could wish to have, we are engirt with foes by land and sea and lack the bare necessities of life. No succour comes to us by ship, nor if such succour came would it avail, for the avenues of aid are closed by a hostile fleet.

Fitz-Stephen, too, whose gallant soul and noble enterprise opened a path for us into this land, is hemmed in by a vindictive race, isolated, and confined within the bulwark of a frail fort of mud and sticks. What then are we to look for? Is it for help from our countrymen across the channel? Why, they regard us no less as Irishmen than we do the besiegers you see around our walls. It would be hard to say whether in that island or in this we are held in greater hate. Away with hesitation, then! Away with cowardice! 'Fortune befriends the venturesome!'* Let us, therefore, sally out upon the enemy like men, while our failing stock of food still gives us strength to do so! A few bold hearts, a few stout arms well trained to wield the sword, hearts that know but how to dare, arms that have carved but a record of victory in the past,—these can crush to powder whole multitudes of an ill-armed, craven rabble such as that which sits about our gates.'

> Such words he utters in impassioned tone;
> And though sore sick at heart with anxious care,
> Yet feigns a cheerfulness he cannot feel:
> Hope on his brow, deep in his breast despair.†

When Maurice closed his speech, Reimund, who felt as keenly as he the same anxiety, spoke at some length amid general applause to a similar effect. He added, too, that they should direct their chief attack upon the king of Connaught, as being pre-eminently the leader of the native force; since, if he were worsted, they would have little difficulty in dealing with the other divisions of the blockading host.‡

(Regan says that the earl was inclined to an accommodation with Roderic, and proposed to hold Leinster of him in fee, but that archbishop Laurence, who was sent to negociate with the Irish, brought back terms too hard to accept, and then Milo de Cogan recommended a sally. According to the same authority this siege of Dublin took place before the assault by Hasculf.)

---

* Verg. Æn. x. 284. † Verg. Æn. i. 208.
‡ These orations (see below, Gerald, II. 13) are, of course, imaginary.

A.D. 1171.—The sally from Dublin.

Regan's Anglo-Norman Poem, ll. 1877-1955.

Such grievous terms unto the earl
    The great archbishop brake;
But Cogan, ever blithe of heart,
    Upsprang and roundly spake:
'A goodly tale of horse and foot,
    Sirs barons, have we here;
Then silent lead we our array
Yon rabble rout to sweep away;
    God helps not those who fear.'
Straight forty cavaliers turned out
    With Milo in the van,
A hundred spears and sixty bows,
    His vassals to a man.
And hard behind Big Reimund * came
    With forty horsemen more,
And eke a hundred men-at-arms,
    And archers thrice a score.
To close the rear, with Strigul's earl
    A forty knights there rode,
A hundred veteran lances too,
    And sixty bowmen strode.
Well found, in sooth, that soldiery
    In garniture of might:
The sun-ray glanced on shield and helm,
    On glaive and hauberk bright.
Now when the good earl's trusty train
    Had cleared the barbican,

---

* "Reimund le Gros" in the text.

THE SALLY.

From column all to line outwheeled,
  Ere the advance began.
The foreguard still, two hundred strong,
  Did bold de Cogan head;
As many more Big Reimund next
  The central battle led.
And last brought up the triple rank
  Two hundred soldiers tall,
Well proved retainers of the earl:
  Six hundred men in all.
And side by side with Milo went
  (So sings the ballad old),
Donnell Kavenagh Dermot's son,
  Anlaf,* O'Reilly of Tirbrun,
  Of whom before we told.
No wit, nor bode of coming doom †
  Had Rory's ‡ savage horde,
Nor spied, nor heard the iron troop,
  That noiseless trode the sward.
For Finglas right, with purpose prompt,
  De Cogan led the way,
For there O'Connor's camp was set:
  Each heart beat high and gay.
With evensong § the band drew near
  To where the siegers lay;
When sharp de Cogan's hest rang out,
  That gave the word to slay.

* Anlaf O'Carvi.
† The Irish expected no attack, especially as there had been some skirmishing that morning.
‡ Roderic. § Gerald, I. 24.

'Strike, strike, in name of Holy Cross,
  Strike, barons, tarry not;
In name of Jesu, Mary's Son,
  Death, death to Erse and Scot.'
Then lord and liegeman, o'er the fence,
  Burst into hut and tent,
And bravely beat the quarters up,
  And smote till they were spent.
Thrust out pellmell the Irish host
  In panic poured away;
And over the western wild they spread,
  As scattered sheep might stray.

* * * * *

At prime we numbered of the kerne
  Full fifteen hundred dead;
While stricken of our Englishrie
  A single footman bled.

A.D. 1171.—The treacherous capture of Fitz-Stephen.

Girald. Cambr. Expug. Hibern. Lib. I. cap. xxv.

But the whirligig of Fortune is ever varying prosperity with disaster : Fortune who can be an enduring friend to no man, who wills not that there fall to any on this earth a stable and a perfect happiness. And so in the mean time the men of Wexford, with those of Kenceleia, being together about 3000, treating with contempt the claims of honour and the obligations of the pledges they had sworn, came unexpectedly upon Fitz-Stephen, who had apprehended nothing of the sort, shut him up in his fort* with five men-at-arms and a few archers and harassed him with incessant assaults. But the besieged, although a mere handful, showed the greatest readiness in repelling their attacks, and one William Not, a man-at-arms, especially distinguished himself in the defence. Whereupon, finding that force availed them nothing, the Irish had recourse to their usual weapons of cunning and deceit. Bringing, therefore, up to the entrenchments two bishops, those of Wexford and Kildare, and other persons attired in sacred vestments, they all took their corporal oaths† upon certain holy relics that Dublin had fallen; that the earl, Maurice, Reimund, and every Englishman there had been slain; and that the host of Connaught, in conjunction with that of Leinster, was already marching upon Wexford. They protested, too, that they were acting in the best interests of Fitz-Stephen in offering terms; that, since he had been a kindly and liberal prince to them, they only desired to give him and his garrison a safe passage across to Wales before the arrival of the great army of his bitter enemy the high-king. To these asseverations Fitz-Stephen at length yielded credence, and entrusted himself and his followers to their good faith. Nevertheless they at once set upon the Englishmen, slaughtered some outright, and cruelly entreating others with stripes or wounds, bound them and flung

* At "The Crag." He had sent thirty-six of his men to the assistance of the earl at Dublin (*Regan*).

† *i.e.* swore touching with the hand the Gospels, a crucifix, or some relic.

D

them into prison. But immediately afterwards fame on speeding wing brought the true news of the discomfiture of the besiegers at Dublin and of the advance of the earl. Whereupon the traitors lost no time in setting fire to the whole city with their own hands, and ferried themselves with all their families, goods, and captives over to the island of Begeri, which lay in the mouth of the harbour and is also called Holy Isle.

A description of the earl.

Girald. Cambr. Expug. Hibern. Lib. I. cap. xxvii.

As for the earl personally, he was a man with reddish hair and freckled face, bright gray eyes, delicate, even feminine, features, a high voice and a short neck. Beyond this there was nothing much to remark except his stature, which was above the average. He was a free-handed man, and mild of disposition. What exertion could not effect he attained by suavity of speech. In private life he was more ready to be led by others than to lead. In time of peace he appeared less like a general than like an ordinary soldier; yet in war he was rather a tactician than a fighting man. If supported by the advice of his subordinates, he would dare anything, but he never relied on his own judgment so far as to take the initiative in ordering an attack, and he never of his own inclination staked all on mere personal valour. During an engagement, where his standard waved, there was ever a firm rallying point or a safe refuge for his men. In victory and in defeat he displayed the same equanimity, the same unwavering purpose: by the former he was not puffed up, in the latter he did not despair.

A.D. 1171.—[How the Irish fanned the king's jealousy with complaints against Strongbow.]

Gervas. Cantuar. 1171.

Finally he [*the earl*] gained possession of the fair city of Dublin, and began to cruelly harass the natives. Wherefore the kings and inhabitants of the land were roused to wrath, and by frequent attacks did all they could to drive away their oppressors. But finding it impossible to prevail over soldiers who, although fewer in number than themselves, were braver and more skilful, they sent ambassadors to the king of England to pray him to come into Ireland and by taking over the lordship of the country himself to relieve them from the insolence and tyranny of earl Richard.

A.D. 1171.—Of the meeting of the earl with the king of the English.

Girald. Cambr. Expug. Hibern. Lib. I. cap. xxviii.

On receipt of these tidings,[*] they turned rein to the right in great bitterness of heart and took the road to Waterford. There they found Hervey, just returned

---

[*] The news of the capture by treachery of Fitz-Stephen at "The Crag," coupled with a message that any attempt at rescue would be met by the instant decapitation of the prisoners.

from his mission to the king of the English: he bore letters, and a verbal message as well, inviting the earl also to go to England. So the latter, as the wind was favourable, at once crossed the water and found the king at Newnham in Gloucestershire, fully prepared to pass over with a considerable army. There, after a good deal of altercation, the royal anger against the earl was, through the address and mediation of Hervey, at length appeased, on the understanding that he should renew his oath of fealty and give up to the king the chief city of Ireland, that is Dublin, together with its adjacent hundreds, and also the maritime towns and all castles. The rest of his conquests he and his heirs were to recognize as held of the king and his successors The question having been settled on these terms, the king set out along the coast road leading to St. David's,* and reaching Pembrokeshire soon got together a gallant fleet in Milford Haven.

(Meanwhile O'Ruarc, king of Meath, taking advantage of the absence of the earl, made an attack on Dublin, which Milo de Cogan defeated by another sally. On the 18th October the English king reached Waterford with 400 ships carrying 500 knights,† 4000 men-at-arms, and several thousand archers.)

---

* The same road as that taken by the earl [chap. xvi. of Gerald above]. Hanmer states that at this time Strongbow's possessions in England and Normandy were restored to him by the king. His authority is the Chronicles of Conway Abbey.

† Many of the men-at-arms who were employed in the conquest of Ireland were Flemish mercenaries, "Brabanters." In fact in this war we find in motley collision Anglo-Norman, Fleming, Brythonic Kelt, Goidelic Kelt, Iberian, and Norseman.

Girald. Cambr. Expug. Hibern. Lib. 1. cap. xxx.

* * * * *

Then was fulfilled that prophecy of Merlin the Wild :—

> From out the distant East a fiery star shall rise,
> Full in whose fatal path foredoomed Hibernia lies.

And that of Moling the Erseman :—

> From the yawning gates of the blood-red morn
> Outpoureth the whirlwind's rush,
> Which hasting ever its Westward course
> Ivernia's life shall crush.

* * * * *

(While Henry II. was yet at Waterford, the men of Wexford in order to curry favour with him, placed in his hands their prisoner Fitz-Stephen, complaining that he had been the first to establish for his countrymen a precedent for invading Ireland without the permission of their over-lord the English king. Henry, probably partly to conciliate the natives, partly to make a show of his authority over the Norman adventurers in Ireland, sent him off, still a prisoner, to Reginald's Tower, but soon after released him. The kings of Desmond and Thomond now voluntarily came to make formal submission to Henry, who appointed his own officers over their respective capitals, Cork and Limerick. Other chiefs of South Ireland followed the example thus set ; as also, when the king went to Dublin after the Synod of Cashel, did those of Leinster and Meath and one of the lords of Uriel. Finally the kigh-king Roderic acknowledged him as over-lord, though he was reluctant to do so.)

Gervas. Cantuar. 1171.

For he [*Roderic*] said that the whole of Ireland was rightly his, and that all the other kings of that land ought to be placed under his authority.

(But even when he did submit he would not go in person to the English king.)

Radulph. de Dicet. Ymag. Hist. 1171.

But Roderic, the kinglet of Connaught, relying on the natural defences of that province, did not condescend to come and meet the English monarch. For his territory is rendered inaccessible by the immense swamps which lie along its borders and present no convenient fords, are nowhere bridged over, and are unsafe for boats.

(The princes of Ulster alone held aloof. The title assumed by the English king was lord of Ireland, and so it remained till the reign of Henry VIII.)

[Nov. 6th] A.D. [1171 or] 1172.—The Synod of Cashel.

Girald. Cambr. Expug. Hibern. Lib. I. cap. xxxiv.

The island was now tranquil in the presence of the king, and enjoyed the blessings of peace and rest. Moved, therefore, by zeal for the advancement of the glory of the Church of God and the honour of Christ in those parts, he summoned a synod of all the clergy of Ireland to meet at Cashel. A public inquiry was there made into the evil ways and foul lives of the people of that land, and the evidence carefully reduced to writing under the seal of the legate of Lismore,[*] who by virtue of his office presided over the assembly. Wherefore the synod enacted many godly constitutions, which are still extant, touching the contracting of marriages, the payment of tithes, the reverence due

[*] Christian, bishop of Lismore from 1150 to 1175, and at this time papal legate as well.

THE ROCK OF CASHEL. From a Water colour Drawing by Thomas Girtin, *circa* 1795; in the possession of the Editor.

to sacred buildings, and of regular attendance thereat. These canons the king published with the object of assimilating the Church of Ireland in all respects to the discipline of the Anglican Church.

Rog. Houeden. Chron. [1171 or] 1172.

I. At this synod it was ordained that children should be brought to the churches and be there baptized in clean water with three immersions, in the name of the Father, the Son, and the Holy Ghost. And that this be done by priests, unless, through fear of death intervening, it be expedient that the ceremony be performed by a person other than a priest and elsewhere than in a church. And that in such case the function may be discharged by any one, irrespective of sex or calling.

Benedict. Abbat. gest. reg. Hen. II. 1171 [or 1172].

For before that time it had been the custom in divers parts of Ireland for the newly born infant to be thrice dipped by its father, or anybody else, in milk ; * while such milk or water that might be thus used was then thrown into the drains or some other unclean place.

Rog. Houeden. Chron. [1171 or] 1172.

II. & III. Item that tithes of all possessions be paid to the churches. Item that all laics who may

* Possibly a relic of some ancient pagan or medical custom. Campion says that even at his day in some parts of Ireland the right arm was left unchristened, "that it might give a more ungracious and deadly blow."

desire to take wives shall do so according to ecclesiastical law.

Benedict. Abbat. gest. reg. Hen. II. 1171 [*or.* 1172].

For most of them were accustomed to have as many wives as they wished, and would even wed their nearest relatives.

Girald. Cambr. Expug. Hibern. Lib. I. cap. xxxv.

IV. That all church lands and possessions be entirely exempt from imposts by secular men. And especially that neither the native kinglets [*reguli*], nor the royal earls, nor any magnates of Ireland, nor their sons and households, shall exact provisions and lodging in ecclesiastical territory as the custom has been, nor henceforward presume to extort such by violence. And that the detestable practice followed by the earls of taking purveyance from the neighbouring ecclesiastical towns four times yearly be in future wholly discontinued.

V. That in the case of composition for homicide by laics, clerks, though of kin to them, shall in no wise contribute thereto; but as they were free of share in the deed, so shall they be free of share in the payment therefor.

VI. That all good Christian men who may be taken with sickness shall in the presence of their confessors and neighbours make their last solemn testaments in due form. That the movable goods of any such, if he have wife and offspring, (debts and wages being first deducted) be divided into three parts. Of these he shall bequeath one to his children, another to his wife, being lawful, and the third to such purpose as he may declare. And if haply he have not legitimate issue, then shall his goods be divided in equal shares between himself * and his wife. And if his wife, being lawful, shall have predeceased him, in that case the property shall be apportioned to himself * and to his children in two equal lots.

VII. That to those who may depart this life after good confession due obsequies be paid, with masses, vigils, and burial rites.

Thus all sacred offices shall henceforth be universally performed in conformity with the usage of the Holy Catholic Church as observed by the Anglican Church. For it is right and just that as Heaven has allotted to Ireland a lord and king from England, so also the former island should receive therefrom an amended mode of life. In truth it is to this magnificent king that both church and state in Ireland owe whatever accession of peace and religion they have so far gained; since before his coming into that country all sorts and kinds of wickedness had sprung up there through a long period of time, which by his authority and care have now been done away with.

Rog. Houeden. Chron. [1171 or] 1172.

The king of England, further, sent a copy of the charters of all the archbishops and bishops of Ireland to pope Alexander [iii], and the holy father himself

---

* *i.e.* for his residuary legatees; *cf.* Coronation Charters of Henry I. and Stephen.

58 CHARTERS GRANTED TO DUBLIN. 1171 or 1172

by the apostolic authority confirmed to him and to his heirs the kingdom of Ireland according to the tenour of the charters of the archbishops and bishops of that land.

After these transactions had been finally completed at Waterford, the king of England went on thence to Dublin, and stayed there from the feast of St. Martin * till the beginning of fast-tide [*Lent*]. While in that place he had built for him, hard by the church of the Apostle St. Andrew, outside the city of Dublin, a royal palace, constructed with marvellous skill of smoothed osiers [*wattled work*] after the manner of that country. In this he himself, with the kings and princes of Ireland, held the usual festivities on the anniversary of the Nativity of our Lord.

(The Irish hierarchy at this time numbered four archbishops and twenty-eight or twenty-nine bishops [*see Table at end*]. The archbishops present at the synod were those of Cashel, Dublin, and Tuam ; but Gelasius, the venerable primate of Armagh, then over eighty years of age, was too infirm to join the assembly. He came on afterwards, however, to Dublin to signify his assent to the constitutions, attended as usual by his white cow, the milk of which formed his only nourishment.† The synod had practically acknowledged the English king as over-lord of Ireland.)

A.D. 1171 or 1172.—[First Dublin] Charter of Henry II.

Archives of the City of Dublin.

Henry, king of England, duke of Normandy and Aquitaine, and count of Anjou, to his archbishops,

* "St. Martin in the winter : " Nov. 11th.
† He was canonized after death ; his day being March 27th.

bishops, abbots, earls, barons, justices, sheriffs, officers, and all liegemen, French, English, and Irish, of all his land, greeting:

Know ye that I have given and granted and by the present charter confirmed to my men of Bristol my city of Dublin to dwell in.

Wherefore I will, and steadfastly enjoin, that they have and hold it of me and of my heirs, well and in peace, freely and undisturbed, entirely and fully and honourably, with all liberties and free customs which the men of Bristol have in Bristol and throughout all my land.

Witnesses: William de Braos; Reginald de Curtenai; Hugh de Gundeville; William Fitz-Aldelm; Ralph de Glanville; Hugh de Creissi; Reginald de Pavilli. At Dublin.

A.D. 1171 or 1172.—[Second Dublin] Charter of Henry II.

Archives of the City of Dublin.

Henry, king of England, duke of Normandy and Aquitaine, and count of Anjou, to his archbishops, bishops, abbots, earls, barons, justices, sheriffs, and all men of his land greeting:

Know ye that I have granted to my burgesses of Dublin that they be exempt from import duties, ferry-tolls, bridge-tolls, lading-dues, paving-rates, mural-rates,* export duties, cart-service, and all customs

* For the maintenance of the fortifications of the city.

throughout my realm of England, Normandy, Wales, and Ireland, wherever they or their goods may go.

Wherefore I will and steadfastly enjoin that they have all their liberties, quittances, and free customs fully and honourably, as being my free and faithful men, and that they be exempt from import duties, ferry-tolls, bridge-tolls, lading-dues, paving-rates, mural-rates, export duties, cart-service, and every other custom. And I forbid that any man molest them in this matter contrary to my charter on pain of a fine of ten pounds.

Witnesses : Richard de Humet, constable ; Reginald de Curtenay; Richard de Camville; William de Lanvaley. At St. Lo.

A.D. 1171 or 1172.—Of the storms.

Girald. Cambr. Expug. Hibern. Lib. I. cap. xxxvi.

Then were the barriers of the storm-winds burst and the bowels of the sea uptorn ; and with such force and for so long did the tempest's rage endure, that the whole drear winter through scarce a single bark found its way across to Ireland, nor could aught of news be heard from any source. Wherefore all men thought that the wrath of God was upon them for their sins.

It was about that time that from the unusual violence of the weather the sand on the shores of South Wales was washed away and the under soil laid bare, and the face of the coast was revealed as it had been in the far distant past. Trunks of trees appeared below high-water mark, still standing, but with their branches broken off or lopped, and showing traces of the axe as if of yesterday. The soil too was quite black, and the wood of the dead tree-boles was of the hue of ebony. Wondrous the changes wrought by time: that where in former days tall ships could ride, now no ship can go; where was a level strand, we see a sylvan grove! Perchance during the flood of Noah, but likelier long since that, though yet in ages long ago, this forest was broken down by the fury of the sea, and by degrees destroyed or absorbed as the waters rose from time to time and encroached upon the land.*

Meanwhile the king lingered at Wexford, anxious to hear tidings of his dominions over sea.†

* * * * *

(At length the wind changed to the east, and the king got his news from England. The two papal legates who had been sent to compound for the murder of Becket had reached Normandy, and as this was a pressing matter he had to leave Ireland at once [*Easter Monday, April* 17*th*, 1172] without waiting to build

---

* One may see these ancient stumps of trees to-day in Swansea Bay, and in other parts of Wales. Gerald's description is absolutely accurate. The black soil is also still there, and probably represents what is left of the foliage, branches, smaller trees and undergrowth.

† It is possible, however, that Henry was not sorry, for the excuse afforded by the turbulent weather to remain for a time where he was. He could hardly wish to meet the papal legates who were on their way to investigate the murder of Becket, before the advent of the additional friendly legates who had been sent on afterwards to absolve him.

along the border of the English Pale the chain of castles he had planned in accordance with the usual policy of the Normans and Angevins in a conquered country. Before sailing he made grants of land within the Pale in fee to his English vassals, in such a way that side by side with the original adventurers there should be settled men on whom he could personally rely. Strongbow was appointed marshal of Ireland and earl of Leinster; Hugh de Laci justiciar and constable of the realm, with the earldom of Meath and with Dublin as his capital. This munificent grant to de Laci was intended by the king as a set-off against the influence of Strongbow. In the following year Reimund Fitz-Gerald was nominated by Henry at Strongbow's request as coadjutor to the latter.)

A.D. 1172.—[Grant of Meath to Hugh de Laci.]

Translated from the text quoted in Spencer's View of the State of Ireland.

Henry by the grace of God king of England, duke of Normandy and Aquitaine, and count of Anjou to his archbishops, bishops, abbots, earls, barons, justices, and all officers and liegemen French, English, and Irish of all his land greeting. Know ye that I have given and granted and by my present charter confirmed to Hugh de Laci for his service the land of Meath with all its purtenances for the service of fifty knights, to him and his heirs to have and to hold of me and my heirs, as Murchard Hu-Melathlin * held it, or any other before or after him. And as an addition to that grant all the fees which he hath granted or shall grant around Dublin, so long as he is my bailiff, for doing service to me at my city of

* The then king of Meath, who was thus dispossessed.

Dublin. Wherefore I will and steadfastly enjoin that Hugh himself and his heirs after him have the aforesaid land, and hold all liberties and free customs which I have or can have there on the service aforesaid of me and of my heirs, well and in peace, freely, undisturbed, and honourably, in wood and plain, in meadow and pasture, in waters and mills, in fishponds and pools, and fisheries, and hunting-grounds, in ways and byways, and seaports, and in all other places and things pertaining thereto, with all liberties which I have there or am able to give and by this my charter confirm to him. Witnesses: earl Richard Fitz-Gilbert; William de Braose; etc. At Wexford.

Sept. 30th, A.D. 1172.—[Letter from pope Alexander III. to the Irish bishops.]

No. 38 in the Calendar of Documents relating to Ireland, 1172.

"Pope Alexander [iii] to Christian, bishop of Lismore, legate of the apostolic see, Gelasius, archbishop of Armagh, Donatus, archbishop of Cashel, Laurence, archbishop of Dublin, Catholicus, archbishop of Tuam, and their suffragans. Having gathered from their letters that the king of England instigated by divine inspiration had subjected to his dominion the Irish people, and that illicit practices began to cease, the pope returns thanks to Him who had conferred so great a victory. Exhorts them to aid the king in governing Ireland and to smite with ecclesiastical censure any of its kings, princes, or people who shall dare to violate the oath and fealty they have sworn. Frascati : ij Kal. Octob'. [*Black Book Exchequer*, Q.R. fo. 8. b.]."

A.D. 1172.—Of the treachery and death of O'Ruarc, [king of Meath].

Girald. Cambr. Expug. Hibern. Lib. I. cap. xli.

Meanwhile, under the governors appointed by the king, Ireland had breathing-time and peace, when it happened in the Dublin district that a conference was arranged between Hugh de Laci and O'Ruarc the One-eyed, king of Meath, an exact time and place being fixed. But during the night preceding the day selected for the meeting, one Griffith, a man-at-arms, and nephew of Maurice [Fitz-Gerald] and Fitz-Stephen, had a dream in which he saw a herd of wild boars rushing in a body upon Hugh and Maurice; and the largest and fiercest, the leader of the drove, was on the point of transfixing them with its tusks, when the sleeper brought his stout arm to their assistance and slew the beast.

On the morrow they set out for the appointed spot, which is called the Hill of O'Ruarc.* Arrived there, the parties first halted at a distance from each other and mutually sent messengers; then on receiving pledges and making oath on either side, they joined for the parley. By previous agreement those that met

* This was probably only a temporary name arising out of the incident narrated in this chapter. It was generally known as the Hill of Tlachtgha, now the Hill of Ward, near Athboy in Meath. The Four Masters say that the treachery was on the part of the English.

were very few and equal in number, and unarmed, except that the English bore their swords, the Irish their axes. The rest of their respective followers stayed some little distance apart from them. But Griffith, who had attended in the train of Maurice, being very anxious about his vision of the night before, had in consequence of it picked out from among his own kinsmen seven men-at-arms in whose valour he had especial confidence, and drawn them to one side of the hill, but as near to the talkers as was allowed. They then adjusted their shields, set lance in rest, and giving rein to their chargers, made a show of tilting after the French fashion, to the intent that however the colloquy should end this pretence of sport might enable them to be ready for any emergency. Meanwhile there had been some hot altercation between O'Ruarc and Hugh de Laci touching the questions in dispute, and matters were tending rather to an aggravation of the discord between them than to a settlement, when the one-eyed villain, meditating in his heart a fell act of treachery, made an excuse for going aside for a moment and gave a sign to his men to come up at once with all speed. This done, he turned and strode hurriedly back, with raised axe, and face white with passion. But Maurice Fitz-Gerald had chanced to hear of the dream from his nephew, and being thereby put on his guard, had carefully watched all O'Ruarc's movements, and had sat during the whole consultation with his sheathed sword lying ready across his knees and his hand on the hilt. He now whipped it out, and with a hasty word of warning to

E

Hugh, boldly started up to defend him. The traitor then aimed a desperate blow at de Laci, but it fell on the interpreter: he, faithful servant, had interposed himself between his master and the stroke, which lopped off his arm and inflicted a fatal wound. Maurice now shouted to his comrades for aid, and in the mean time, while sword encountered battle-axe, in the hurry of the retreat Hugh twice stumbled to the ground, and effected his escape with difficulty and then only with Fitz-Gerald's aid.

While this was going on, the Irish, who, in obedience to the caitiff's signal, had appeared in large numbers from the neighbouring hollows, were quickly running in from all directions with their pairs of javelins and their great axes, and would soon have made an end of Maurice and Hugh had not Griffith and his companions, attracted by the cries of the former, ridden up at a gallop. On seeing this O'Ruarc thought it well to look to himself and seek safety in flight; but while he was in the very act of mounting a horse which had been led to him, Griffith got up just in time to run his lance through man and steed together. With him were killed on the same spot three of his attendants who had risked their lives in bringing him the horse. His head was cut off and afterwards sent over to the king of the English, even into England. The ▪remainder of the natives fled in confusion and scattered over the plain, but a vast slaughter was made of them and continued even till they reached the far distant woods. Ralph, son of Fitz-Stephen, a stout and daring youth, earned especial credit that day for vigour and courage.

A.D. 1172.—[The death of O'Ruarc: An Irish account].

Annals of Ulster; 1172: *Translated from the Irish by an unknown hand; in MS.*

"Tiernan O'Ruarc, king of Breifny and [East Meath], a man of great power for a long time, was killed by the English and by Donnell . . . of his own kindred, and being by them beheaded they carried his head and body miserably to Dublin. His head was hanged up upon the gate of the city. The body was buried in another place with his [*sic*] feet upward."

A description of Maurice [Fitz-Gerald].

Girald. Cambr. Expug. Hibern. Lib. I. cap. xliii.

Maurice was a man of unassuming but dignified bearing; his features regular, his complexion embrowned by exposure; of medium height, neither above nor below the average. As with his stature, so it was with his temperament; moderation was the characteristic of each: the former showed no disproportion, the latter no extravagance. Nature had made him a worthy man, and he cared more to be so than to seem so. His efforts were always directed to observing the happy mean in everything, and with such success that for uprightness and for refined courtesy he may be considered the best example as he was the pattern of his country and his times. A man of few words, but what he had to say was terse and well put: for he set more store by heart than tongue, placed reason above eloquence, regarded wisdom rather than words. Yet when there was need of oratory, though deliberate in delivering his opinion, he could express himself with polished skill. In war he was full of courage, and second to hardly any one in vigour of action; at the same time not impetuous or apt to run headlong into danger. Wary, however, as he was in attack, he was equally resolute in defence. In him temperance, discretion, and chastity were combined with stability of character, firmness, and good faith. A man not indeed faultless, still free from any actual vice or sin.

A description of Henry II., king of the English.

Girald. Cambr. Expug. Hibern. Lib. 1. cap. xlvi.

I have thought it not improper to pourtray for the benefit of posterity the appearance and the character of the king, his peculiarities of person and of mind: so that those who in future ages may love to hear of the great deeds he wrought, may also picture him to themselves as he looked and was.

*   *   *   *   *

It would be pleasant indeed, though I fear beyon my powers, to be able to tell the whole truth abou a prince without offending him.

Well, Henry II., king of the English, was a man with reddish hair, a big bullet-head, blood-shot gray eyes that in anger flashed fiercely, a fiery face, and a broken voice. He had a bull neck, a square chest,

SEAL OF HENRY II., FROM ORIGINAL IN BRITISH MUSEUM.

muscular arms, and a fleshy body, which last was due rather to natural tendency than to the over-gratification of his appetite at table; his figure was portly, but not absolutely of huge and unwieldy bulk, thanks to a certain limit which he observed even in his excesses. For he was abstemious in food and temperate in drink, and, so far as a prince could be, in everything inclined to be frugal. Nay, in order to do all he could to check and minimize this injustice of nature and by force of will counteract his constitutional inclination to corpulence, just as though he had conspired against himself to wage an intestine war with his belly, it was his custom to harass his body by excessive exercise. So not only when war was going on—and that was very often—would he scarcely allow himself for rest the few hours that were not devoted to business, but even in time of peace there was no repose for him. For he was attached beyond measure to the pleasures of the chase, and he would start off the first thing in the morning on a fleet horse, and now traversing the woodland glades, now plunging into the forest itself, now crossing the ridges of the hills, used in this way to pass day after day in tireless toil; and when in the evening he reached home, he was rarely seen to sit down whether before or after supper. In spite of all the fatigue he had undergone, he would keep the whole court standing till they were worn out. But, as the adage says, 'To observe the happy mean in everything is the first rule in life,' * and since even a remedy if carried to excess ceases

* Ter. *And.* I. i. 34.

to be beneficial, these habits, by inducing frequent swellings of the feet and lower leg, which were aggravated by the restive motions of the high-spirited horses he rode, brought on further disorders; and, if they did no other harm, they certainly hastened the approach of old age, the origin and promoter of all the ills of corporeal humanity.

As for his stature, he was of medium height; and in this he differed from all his sons, for the two elder were somewhat taller, the two younger shorter, than most men.

In his unruffled moods, and when not excited by anger, he was remarkably eloquent, and, as came out at such times, well learned. An affable man, too, who could be influenced, though of a ready wit; indeed, he was second to no one in courtesy, whatever the real sentiments his outward bearing might conceal.

He was a prince of such admirable religious sense that whenever he conquered in battle, it was only to be overcome in turn by his gratitude to Heaven. Though strenuous in war, he prudently tried to avoid it when at peace; for during hostilities he always had a wholesome apprehension of the uncertainty of the issue, and from his extreme caution he would, in the words of the comic poet, 'try all means rather than resort to arms.'* Those whom he lost in fight, he mourned as princes rarely do, and showed greater tenderness of feeling for the fallen than for the survivors: he was far less demonstrative in his care for the living than in his grief for the dead. No one was

* Ter. *Eun.* iv. 7. 19.

kinder in the hour of trouble: when all was well again, no one more severe.

Harsh the king is to the lawless; clement he to lowly hearts:
Strict within his halls; yet harb'ring strangers from outlandish parts:
Bounteous in the outer world; at home instilling thrifty arts.

The man for whom he had once conceived a hate, he could with difficulty be brought to love; where once he had set his affections, rarely did his regard change to dislike.

He rejoiced in the sport of falconry; it gladdened him to watch the flight of the fierce hawk. He loved, too, beyond measure to hear the baying of the pack as they sped on the scent of the hunted deer. I could wish that he had cultivated as diligently the offices of religion as he did the pleasures of the field. His belief that the grievous injuries offered him by his sons had sprung from the instigation of the queen, led him after their revolt to live in open violation of his marriage vow. Still he was by nature not a truthful man, and would habitually break his word without the slightest excuse. For whenever he found himself in a difficulty he preferred that his honour should suffer rather than his interest, and thought it better to lose his reputation for honesty than to miss an advantage. In the transaction of business he was always so cautious and so circumspect, that for this very reason, carrying his prudence to an extreme, he was dilatory in the administration of justice; and to the great inconvenience of his subjects exceedingly slow in coming to a final decision in any matter.

Moreover, whereas Justice, which is divine, which therefore should be gratuitously rendered without price, which is not a commodity to be purchased by lucre, with us is bought and sold, which itself freely accords all things, with us is held in traffic, he [*the king*] has left behind alike in the state and in the priesthood notorious successors of the iniquitous Gehazi.* He was a lover of peace, and diligent in maintaining it. Of unequalled munificence in alms-giving, he was an especial benefactor to the Holy Land. A lover of humility, he kept a tight hand upon the nobles of his realm and ground under his heel any show of arrogance. Filling the hungry with good things, the rich he sent empty away.†

> He raised the humble from their lowly state,
> And from their seats above debased the great.

In the things that are of God he was guilty of many reprehensible usurpations; and through a zeal for justice—a zeal, however, not tempered by discretion—he confused the rights of the crown with those of the priesthood,‡ to the end that he might stand forth as the sole fount of justice. Son of the church as he was, and owing his crown to her, yet he either forgot or affected to forget the sacramental unction he had received. Scarcely would he spare an hour to attend the holy sacrifice of the mass, and even then so great, forsooth, was the press of public busi-

* Implying that the king was guilty of simoniacal practices.
† Luke i. 53.
‡ That is, he encroached upon the legal privileges of the clergy. The allusion is to the Constitutions of Clarendon (1164).

ness that he spent the time more in discussion and conversation than in prayer. The income of vacant benefices it was his habit to pay into the public treasury; and, since a little leaven corrupts the mass, inasmuch as he thus appropriated to the exchequer the revenues which were due to Christ, being ever plunged in fresh difficulties, he exhausted his coffers again and again.* Thus into the pockets of a profane soldiery went that which was by right the stipend of the clerk.

Of his consummate forethought many a scheme did he conceive, and for the prudent execution thereof he carefully arranged. Still it was not every one that turned out well; he was often disappointed of success. At the same time there was no instance of a great failure which did not originate in some trifling accident.

On his legitimate offspring he bestowed, during their childhood, even more than the natural affection of a father, but as they advanced in years he regarded them with more than the jealousy of a step-father. And for all he had such renowned and illustrious sons, yet this very fact proved a great bar to his complete happiness, in that he always showed aversion towards his possible successors, though perhaps not without reason after their conduct to him. And since human prosperity, just as it is transient, so can never be complete; in like manner by the refined malice, as it were, of Fortune it happened that where the king

* The passage means that he derived no permanent benefit from such ill-gotten gains.

looked for happiness there he found hostility; where defence, defiance; where help, hate; where rest and repose, there especially disquiet and disturbance. It may have been the ill-assorted union of the parents that was to blame, it may have been in punishment for the royal sins : but, however that may be, the fact remains that there was no real concord between the princes and their father, nor harmony among the princes themselves.

At length the pretenders to power and the disturbers of peace were put down both in England and in France, whether it had been brother against brother, son against sire, or vassal against suzerain, and for a long season the king enjoyed all the prosperity he could wish. Would that even then, at the eleventh hour, he had testified by righteous works his appreciation of so convincing a proof of the divine mercy.

Surrounded though he was at all times by crowds of faces, features that he had scanned but once he never forgot. Whatever on any occasion he had heard and thought worth noting, never escaped his memory. Whence he always had available a ready recollection of nearly the whole course of history as well as of most of the facts that his own wide experience had taught him. And to conclude in a few words, had he been one of God's elect and inclined himself to yield obedience to His commands, his natural endowments were such that he would have been unequalled among the princes of the world.

But enough of this topic, which, although by no means foreign to my subject, I have here but briefly and hurriedly touched upon. The above short sketch may suggest to some abler writer than myself a historical theme well worthy of his pen ; and now let me return to my relation of events in Ireland.

(In 1173 we find hostilities again general in Ireland. There were marauding expeditions on the part of the settlers, and counter forays by the natives.; besides a sea-fight in Lismore Haven.)

A.D. 1174.—[Disastrous incursion into Munster by the earl].
Annals of Innisfallen: 1174 ; *O'Donovan's Translation from the Irish.*

" A great army was led by the earl of Strigul to plunder Munster ; and he sent messengers to Dublin desiring all the Galls [*Ostmen*] left there to join him ; and a battalion of knights, officers, and soldiers, well armed came to him, and they all marched to Durlus-O'Fogarty [*Thurles, in N.E. Desmond*]. But Donnell More O'Brien there defeated the earl and the knights, and slew four of the knights and 700 of their men.* When that news came to the hearing of the people of Waterford, they killed the 200 who were guarding the town.† Then the earl went on an island near the town (the Little Island) and remained there for a month."

(A general rising prompted by this success prevented him from moving, and in the meanwhile Roderic of Connaught crossed

---

* Gerald says the earl was surprised early one morning, and that the loss fell mainly on the Ostmen. He states that loss at 400.

† This was done "ab iniquis Ostmannis," says Gerald, so that altogether the Ostmen were not very reliable allies as yet.

the Shannon, burnt the deserted strongholds and laid waste the country up to the walls of Dublin. The earl was, however, then relieved by Reimund, who had been away in Wales but returned with a force on hearing of the peril of his countrymen. The news of the coming of Reimund with his reinforcements was, says Gerald, sufficient to frighten Roderic back again into Connaught, for he had had a foretaste of his valour and ability as a leader at Dublin in 1171, where Reimund had been one of the leaders of the sortie which raised the siege. The rising in Waterford was presently put down.)

1174 or 1175.—The granting of a bull of privileges.

Girald. Cambr. Expug. Hibern. Lib. II. cap. v.

Meanwhile the king of the English, although his time and attention were very much occupied with military affairs, was not forgetful of his realm of Ireland, and sent ambassadors to the court of Rome bearing the evidence which had been carefully collected and taken down at the synod of Cashel touching the evil lives of the inhabitants of that island. Alexander III., who was then pontiff, granted a bull of privileges which conferred upon the English king, with the papal authority and assent, the dominion over the Irish people; and since they were grossly ignorant of the rudiments of the faith, further empowered him to mould them by ecclesiastical rules and discipline to a conformity with the usage of the Anglican Church. . . . A meeting of the bishops was forthwith called at Waterford, at which the bull was formally read in public, and met with general approval. With it was read another bull which the same king had previously procured by means of John

of Salisbury, afterwards bishop of Chartres, from pope
Adrian,* the predecessor of Alexander. John had
been sent to Rome on that business, and by his hands
Adrian had presented the king of the English with a
golden ring in token of the investiture. This ring
together with the bull of Adrian had been deposited
among the archives at Winchester. Wherefore I have
thought it not superfluous to insert here the contents
of that instrument.

[*The bull Laudabiliter.*]

"Adrian the bishop, servant of the servants of God,
to his well-beloved son in Christ the illustrious king
of the English sendeth greeting and the apostolic
benediction. With praiseworthy and profitable zeal
your highness entertaineth a desire of increasing the
glory of your name on earth, and of laying up for
yourself the meed of eternal happiness in heaven. For,
as becometh a Catholic prince, you propose to extend
the boundaries of the church, to make known the
truth of the Christian faith to an unlearned and
savage race, and to root out the weeds of vice from
the garden of the Lord. The better to attain that
end you seek the advice and favour of the apostolic
see. And we are assured that the higher your aim

* Adrian IV. [Nicholas Breakspeare, the only Englishman
who has occupied the papal chair] was pope from 1154 to 1159,
and was the immediate predecessor of Alexander III. There
had been a friendly connection between Henry and Adrian even
before the former became king and the latter pope. This is the
bull known as "Laudabiliter," granted in 1155.

and the greater your discretion in the pursuit of the object you have in view, the more complete, with God's help, will be your success; since an enterprise which hath originated in enthusiasm for religion and in love of our creed will of a surety attain to a happy issue and a noble result. That Ireland and all islands whereon Christ, the Sun of righteousness, hath shed his ray, and which have received the evidence of the truth of Christianity, are in the dominion of the blessed Peter and the Holy Roman Church, your highness acknowledgeth and no one doubteth.* Wherefore we are the readier to implant in them the seeds of a faith which shall be acceptable to God, and yet the more so inasmuch as we know that the day of scrutiny will come when a strict reckoning of our stewardship will be required of us. Whereas, then, you our well-

---

* This claim was founded on what is known as the "Donatio Constantini." Although not questioned in the middle ages, this Donation is now regarded as a forgery. According to it the first Christian emperor [Constantine I., "The Great"], who reigned from A.D. 309 to 337, in gratitude for the cure of his leprosy through the prayers of pope Sylvester I., granted to him and his successors Italy and the whole West, and transferred the seat of the civil power to the Bosphorus, in order that the ecclesiastical polity should not be hampered by the proximity of secular government. This was one of the germs from which grew the temporal claims of the papacy. The forgery probably dates from about A.D. 775, at which time Adrian I. was pope. The claim was now put forward as applying only to islands to avoid giving offence to the kings of Western Christendom. England was not regarded as an island: but as a kind of "alter orbis" with reference to the continent; much as we look at Australia.

beloved son in Christ have signified to us that you are wishful of entering the island of Ireland, in order to subject its people to the rule of law and to root out therefrom the weeds of vice; and are willing to pay from each house an annual tribute of one penny to the blessed Peter,* and to preserve the rights of the church of that land uncorrupted and intact : We therefore support with due favour your devout and laudable desire, and to your petition accord our gracious assent. It is our will and pleasure that for the extending of the boundaries of the church, the checking of the downward course of crime, the correction of immorality, the engrafting of virtue, and for the glorification of the religion of Christ, you do enter that island and execute therein all things that regard the honour of God and the weal of the aforesaid land; and the people of that land shall receive you with fitting honour and do homage to you as their over-lord. It being provided that the rights of the church remain uncorrupted and intact, and that there be reserved for the blessed Peter and the Holy Roman Church the annual tribute of one penny from every house. If therefore you decide to put into execution the project you have conceived, be it your study to instruct the Irish nation in the ways of virtue ; be it, too, your care that this be carried out under yourself by such persons as you know to be well qualified for the task by reason of their faith, their integrity, and their

* "Peter-pence." But payments to Rome were in England generally regarded not as obligatory taxes or tribute but as alms ("eleemosyna beati Petri").

godly lives. So shall the church among that people be enriched in holiness, so shall the flower of Christian duty be there sown and flourish, and all that pertaineth to the honour of the Almighty and to the salvation of their souls be by you ordered in such fashion that you shall merit at God's hands the inheritance of an eternal reward in the life to come, and on earth shall win a glorious name that will endure for ever."

A.D. 1175.—The famous storming of Limerick.
Girald. Cambr. Expug. Hibern. Lib. II. cap. viL

In the interim Donnell, prince of Limerick, having begun to behave in a most insolent manner, and having repudiated with no less perfidy than disrespect the fealty he had yielded to the king of the English, Reimund collected a force of stout fellows, and about the 1st of October boldly marched to the assault of Limerick with 120 men-at-arms, 300 mounted retainers, and 400 archers on foot. When they reached the Shannon, which flows around that noble city, and found that its deep and rapid stream presented an apparently insurmountable obstacle to their advance, the soldiers, who were thirsting for plunder and renown, felt as though confronted by the waters of Tantalus, and chafed at the impediment which lay between them and the longed-for object so nearly in their grasp. Whereupon a stalwart youth who had lately joined the army, a nephew of Reimund, David Welsh as he was called (though that was not his family name, but indicated his nationality), a stripling of promise, tall and gainly, was even more impatient than his companions; and in his ardent desire for fame, regardless of the danger of a horrible death, plunged into the rushing river with its rough and stony bottom. But by taking the course of the stream obliquely, and by availing himself of the backs of the wavelets, he was carried by his good steed safely across, and called out to his comrades that he had found a ford.

However, as only a single man-at-arms, one Geoffrey Judas, followed his example, he and Judas proceeded to recross at the same place, but the latter was swept away by the impetuosity of the current and perished. On seeing this Meiler, who had come with Reimund, emulous of the intrepid energy and of the daring exploit of David, who was his kinsman, settled himself firmly upon his strong charger and dashed impulsively into the waters. Fired as he was by the zeal of rivalry, and not a whit daunted by the terrible fate he had just witnessed, his confident boldness soon landed him upon the other side.

But some of the citizens met him at the very water-edge, others from the fortifications which commanded the bank hurled volleys of stones and darts, striving either to drive him back, or better still to slay him where he stood. Yet the brave fellow, hemmed in though he was by two unavoidable dangers, here by the furious enemy, there by the raging flood, sturdily held his ground, receiving the missiles on his helmet and his shield.

Reimund, who as commander-in-chief of the army had remained in the rear, was entirely ignorant of what was going on, till the loud shouts that arose from each bank attracted his attention, when he rode hastily up along the lines without drawing rein before he reached the river. Then, seeing his nephew upon the opposite side in so critical a situation, and exposed unsupported to the attacks of the Ostmen, in intense anxiety he cried out sharply to his soldiers: " Men, I know your native spirit, and have tested its mettle in many a strait. Come then, the way has been shown us; this river which seemed impassable, our gallant comrades have proved to be fordable. So, follow we our leaders; let us bear aid to that chivalrous youth who is on the point of being overwhelmed, who made this venture for our common good. Surely we must not allow him to risk his life like this before our eyes!' With these words, he was the first to rush into the stream, followed eagerly by the whole force, thus committing all to fortune. Every one passed unharmed, save only two mounted retainers and one man-at-arms named Guy, who were drowned. The defenders were driven into the city, and the walls at once stormed with a great slaughter of the townsmen. It was a famous capture, and the conquerors, enriched with plenteous spoil and a vast quantity of gold, were compensated by gain and glory for the hazard they had faced.

A description of Reimund [Fitz-Gerald].

Girald. Cambr. Expug. Hibern. Lib. II. cap. viii.

Reimund was a man not much above middle height, but very stout. He had rather curly yellow hair, large round gray eyes, a somewhat high nose, and a sunburnt face of bright and cheerful expression. Although corpulent, the natural vivacity of his temperament seemed to carry off his bulky appearance, and his lively spirits drew away attention from this blemish in his person. In his solicitude for the men under his command he would often pass nights of wakefulness, and as though the watcher of the watchmen, was wont to spend the hours of darkness in anxiously going the rounds from post to post and challenging the sentinels. It was due to his habitual vigilance that troops in his charge very rarely, if ever, got into difficulties either through rash undertakings or through want of care. His tastes were simple and frugal, luxurious neither in point of diet nor of raiment. Patient in trying circumstances, the extremes of heat and cold he bore with equal fortitude, and no toil drew from him a murmur. His duty to his soldiers he held of more account than the personal dignity of his position, and he did not hesitate to appear by his labours for their benefit to be rather their servant than their master. To sum up in brief his merits, character, and habits, he was a man of liberal and kindly heart, but wary and circumspect; and although a dashing and experienced leader, at the same time even in military matters his most distinguishing quality was his prudence. Praiseworthy as a daring soldier, he was yet more to be commended for his consummate caution as a general.

A description of Meiler [Fitz-Henry].
Girald. Cambr. Expug. Hibern. Lib. II. cap. ix.

As for Meiler, he was a swarthy man with fierce black eyes and keen visage. Below the middle height, yet very powerful for one of his stature, he was square chested, and not given to corpulence; his arms, too, and other limbs were long and muscular and free from fat. As a soldier none surpassed him in daring: he shrank from no enterprise, whether it were to be undertaken by his single hand or in company with others. He was the first to plunge into the fight, the last to leave it. Into every engagement he threw his utmost energies, prepared either to vanquish or to die. Such was his headlong eagerness that to achieve the wished-for victory or to meet his end alone did he deem worthy: reckoning there to be no mean between the triumph of a victor and the glory of a soldier's death. So intense his thirst for fame that if perchance it had been denied to him to both conquer and live, he would have chosen conquest even at the price of life.

Both these men would have been deserving of yet higher praise had they subordinated worldly ambition to a becoming reverence for the Church of Christ, by not only preserving inviolate her ancient and veritable rights, but also with laudable liberality contributing as an acceptable peace-offering to God some portion of that newly acquired land which had been gained by the effusion of so much blood and stained by the slaughter of a Christian people. But, indeed, it is greatly to be wondered at, and still more greatly to be lamented that this has unquestionably been a common failing with all our leaders in the Irish war from their first coming down to the present day.

(1175.—Reimund, having provisioned Limerick and placed a garrison there, returned into Leinster. Meanwhile, according to Gerald [II. 10], Hervey de Montmaurice had been privately sending messengers to the king from time to time who played upon the royal fears with malicious statements to the effect that Reimund was aiming at establishing himself as an independent sovereign in Ireland.)

A.D. 1175.—Roderic pays tribute.

Rymer's Foedera. Syllabus ed. Hardy. October 6th 1175.

" Agreement by which Roderic, king of Connaught, being permitted to retain his kingdom consents to become liegeman and to pay tribute [*a tithe of hides*] to the king."

A description of Hervey [de Montmaurice].

Girald. Cambr. Expug. Hibern. Lib. II. cap. xi.

Hervey was a tall, good-looking man, with prominent gray eyes, an engaging presence, pleasing expression of face, and a polished address. His neck was long and thin, too much so, in fact, to properly support his head, and his shoulders were sloping. Conformably to such a figure he had long hands and arms, and a chest only moderately broad. About the waist, where most men are inclined to swell out over much, he was naturally of slight dimensions, so that the lower part of his body was duly proportioned to the width of his breast. But his thigh and lower leg and his feet were well suited to a soldier and harmonized fairly well with the upper part of his frame. His height was above the average. Whatever graces, however, nature had bestowed in the adornment of his personal appearance, she had countervailed by implanting in the inner man many a moral deformity and many a vice. For from youth upwards he had led a life of reprehensible laxity. He was a malignant, a lying tale-bearer, and a double-faced knave. Crafty, plausible, and false, venom tainted the milk and honey of his tongue. His principles were as erratic as his purpose was vague : he was stable in his instability alone. For a time he flourished at the summit of Fortune's wheel; but by a sudden turn he was hurled to the bottom in hopeless ruin. In early life he served with some merit in the French wars; but nowadays he is more remarkable for vindictiveness than for valour, for duplicity than distinction, for impudence than importance, for jests than judgment, for verbosity than for veracity.

(1176.—The king, influenced by the reports of Hervey, recalled Reimund and sent over four commissioners, two of whom were to conduct the latter to England, and two to remain in Ireland with the earl. Just as Reimund was about to leave, news came that Donnell, king of Thomond, had blockaded the English garrison in Limerick.)

A.D. 1176.—Relief of the garrison which had been left at Limerick.

Girald. Cambr. Expug. Hibern. Lib. II. cap. xii.

Reimund was now prepared to start, and only waited for a favourable wind, when, lo! messengers appeared from the garrison of Limerick with tidings that Donnell, prince of Thomond, had blockaded that town with a vast multitude of Irish; and that, since the supplies captured there or brought thither had been consumed during the winter, immediate succour was imperative. Whereupon the earl in his anxiety to send relief, addressed his men on the subject, but found them so gloomy and disheartened at the impending departure of Reimund, that they unanimously refused to move without him.

In this strait a consultation was held with the royal nuncios, and, after some hesitation, Reimund yielded to the urgent request of the earl and the nuncios, and started to march back again on Limerick. As he drew near to Cashel, with 80 men-at-arms, 200 mounted retainers, and 300 archers, besides the Irish auxilaries who accompanied him under Murchard of Kenceleia and Donnell of Ossory, he heard that the men of Thomond had raised the siege and had turned to meet him in the pass of Cashel; and that by felling trees, digging ditches, and running a stiff palisade-work across the road, they had increased the difficulties of a passage difficult enough by nature.

The speech of Donnell [of Ossory].

Girald. Cambr. Expug. Hibern. Lib. II. cap. xiii.

The force was now formed into three divisions, and the men girt themselves for the encounter; when, just as they were approaching the pass, Donnell, prince of the men of Ossory, who had a bitter feud with those of Thomond, struck by the small number of the English troops, though they were splendidly equipped, addressed them in these words:—' Soldiers whose victories have placed this island at your feet, I ask you to display your accustomed bravery in the attack to-day. If your wonted gallantry brings you out victorious again, our axes will back your swords in pressing on the beaten foe; but if my Irishmen see your ranks repulsed, which God forbid, 'tis ten chances to one that they will make common cause with our antagonists and turn upon you. Summon, then, soldiers, all your nerve and wariness: far hence are our cities, far hence our camp, far indeed it were to fly. My countrymen side ever with the winning battalions, are ever ready to fall on those that flee. Trust, therefore, to us for sturdy aid, but only so long as you may keep yourselves unconquered.'

On hearing this, Meiler, who led the first division, threw himself with his men like a mighty whirlwind into the gorge. Down went the stockade, torn away or broken in, utterly destroyed; down, too, its defenders; and a broad path was cloven by the sword through the masses of the enemy behind. Thus was the pass of Cashel forced, and it was on Easter Eve [*Ap.* 3].

Three days later, on Tuesday in Easter week, the triumphant army entered Limerick, being the very day on which the city had been taken before.

After making good the damage sustained by the walls during the blockade, Reimund met the princes of Connaught and Thomond in conference, on the same day, but in different places. Roderic came in a boat on the great lake * which is the source of that noble river the Shannon, whose two branches it sends forth to flow afar through opposite parts of the island to the ocean;† Donnell chose a spot at no great distance from Roderic on the other [*west*] side of the river and at the edge of a certain wood; while Reimund lay between the two, north of Killaloe and about 16 miles from Limerick. The colloquy was prolonged until both princes gave hostages then and there, and in renewing their pledges of good faith to the king of the English and his subjects, took their corporal oaths that in future those pledges should be preserved inviolate.

(We have seen that in this expedition the English had taken advantage of a tribal feud to enlist natives in their service. This policy was continued; indeed we find Irish princes applying to them for aid even against their nearest kinsmen.)

---

* Lough Derg.
† Gerald thought that the Shannon north of Lough Derg was united with Lough Erne, and so joined the sea at Ballyshannon in Donegal Bay.

A.D. 1176.—Concerning the announcement to Reimund of the death of the earl.

Girald. Cambr. Expug. Hibern. Lib. II. cap. xiv.

But while this was doing in Desmond, there came to Reimund an express sent in all haste from Dublin and bearing a missive from his wife Basilia,* though the messenger was ignorant of its contents. The epistle was therefore read to Reimund † in private by a certain clerk of his household, and the purport of it was this :—' To Reimund, her well-beloved lord and spouse, his Basilia wisheth the same health as she hath herself. Be it known to thee my true love, that the great jaw-tooth thou wottest of, the which hath troubled me so much, hath just dropt out. Wherefore if there be any love in thee for me, or even for thyself, see that thou tarry not but hasten thy return.' When these words had been read, Reimund shrewdly guessed that by the falling out of the tooth was indicated the death of the earl. For on setting out he had left the latter lying at Dublin sick of a grave malady. The earl thus died a natural death, and the date was about the 1st of June. Through fear of the Irish, everything was done to keep his decease a secret until the return of Reimund and his force.‡

* Sister of Strongbow.
† Who very probably could not read himself.
‡ So, according to the legends, the news of the death of Tarquinius Priscus was suppressed until Servius Tullius had established his position, and that of the Cid was concealed from the Moors pending the battle of the Navas de Tolosa, in 1099.

Annals of the Four Masters: 1176; *O'Donovan's Translation from the Irish.*

"The English earl died of an ulcer which had broken out in his foot through the miracles of SS. Bridget * and Columbkille, and of all the other saints whose churches had been destroyed by him. He saw, as he thought, St. Bridget in the act of killing him."

(The death of the earl, the situation of Limerick in a remote and hostile district, and his own impending departure for England, decided Reimund, after some hesitation, to evacuate that city, and concentrate the English troops within the Pale.)

A.D. 1176.—[The burning of Limerick and the burial of the earl.]

Girald. Cambr. Expug. Hibern. Lib. II. cap. xiv.

Reimund, finding none among his officers willing to undertake the custody of the city after his departure, entrusted it of his own accord to Donnell of Thomond, as a baron of his lord the king of the English. That chieftain gave fresh hostages, and was profuse in his oaths to preserve the place uninjured, to restore it at the royal command if required so to do, and to keep the peace. But, just as the English were marching out, and when the rear of their column had scarcely passed the further end of the bridge, it was broken

---

* Born about 450, died 525; contemporary with St. Patrick. The saint's day of "the Mary of Erin" is February 1st, and she is remarkable as the patroness of a sacred fire, like that of Vesta at Rome. St. Bridget's fire was duly kept up till the dissolution of monasteries in Henry VIII.'s reign.

down behind them from the town side of the river! They turned, and beheld with grief and vexation that fair city, with its noble walls, its handsome buildings, and its vast store of supplies collected from all the country round, fired in four separate quarters, and given up to the flames. It was the work of the traitor Donnell, who by this new and shameless deed of perfidy, this scandalous instance of foul play, was affording an indication of what sort of confidence should be reposed for the future in the good faith of the Irish race.

The king of the English, on hearing of the above daring march to the assistance of the city, is reported to have said :—'It was a gallant piece of work that attack on Limerick, and its relief still more so : but the evacuation of it afterwards was an act of pure wisdom.'

And so the garrison returned to Dublin, and the body of the earl, which by his own wish had been kept unburied until Reimund's arrival, was entombed with great state in the chancel of the Church of the Holy Trinity [*Christ Church*] at Dublin,* Laurence, the archbishop of that see, officiating at the obsequies.

(In these circumstances the commissioners returned to England for instructions, leaving Reimund to act as "procurator" in Ireland. The king sent over William Fitz-Aldelm, as procurator and justiciary, to take the place of the late earl, and with him came as a coadjutor John de Courci. At this point of his history Gerald gives vent to his anger against the royal officers who had supplanted his relatives the Geraldines.)

---

* Where his tomb, and that of Eva his wife, may still be seen.

Tomb of Strongbow and Eva his Wife in Christ Church Cathedral, Dublin.

Girald. Cambr. Expug. Hibern. Lib. II. cap. xv.

From that hour, then, this fellow [*Fitz-Aldelm*] as well as every other procurator of Ireland through jealousy ceased not as though by a common understanding to harass Reimund, Meiler, the Fitz-Maurices, the Fitz-Stephens and their whole family; though possibly they were prompted to it by instructions from high quarters.* For this seems to have been the destined lot of our house : in times of war ever foremost, ever renowned beyond all for manly enterprise, at such times they were valued as their worth deserved. But when the pinch of necessity was relaxed, straightway they found neglect, abasement, and the hatred which springs from envy. Yet not even the spirit of invidious rivalry could wholly uproot a stock so noble in its nature. Whence even to this day our race, increased and multiplied by fresh offshoots, has no small influence in the island. Who are they who penetrate the strongholds of the foe? The Geraldines. Who are they whose valour holds the conquered land in thrall? The Geraldines. Who are they on whom the trembling foeman looks with dread? The Geraldines. And who are they whose manly worth malicious envy wrongs? The Geraldines. Oh that they had found a prince willing to duly requite their earnest toil! How tranquil, how full of true peace would have been the state of Ireland under their control! But their energy always evoked unreasonable suspicion, while those to whom a misplaced

* The king.

confidence has entrusted the charge of the country afford but a blind security which is based on no foundation.

Yet my glorious and gallant kinsmen, ye who despise the sweets of life but love laborious days, falter not, go forward still on the path of virtue that you have ever trod—

Blest in your manly worth proclaimed if aught my lines avail.*

A description of Fitz-Aldelm.

Girald. Cambr. Expug. Hibern. Lib. II. cap. xvi.

This Fitz-Aldelm was a stout man, yet neither in height nor build much above the ordinary size. His tastes were sumptuous, his manners those of a courtier. But whenever he was unusually polite, you might be sure that he had some snare or trick on hand. In the honey he offered there was poison; the snake in the grass was the type of his mind. Without he appeared an open-hearted and kindly man, but within—

There was more gall than honey in his soul.†

Always he—

Wears placid and fair-seeming brow, and greets with smiles and smirks,
While hidden in his hollow heart the fox's cunning lurks.‡

---

* Verg. *Æn.* ix. 446. [On or about 1st September, 1176, died Maurice Fitz-Gerald, at Wexford.]

† Juv. vi. 181.
‡ Persius, v. 116. } Gerald's quotations are not verbatim.

Always he—

> Proffers some deadly draught in cup with honied rim.*

"His words were softer than oil, Yet were they drawn swords." † Those whom to-day he treated with respect, to-morrow he would calumniate or plunder. A bully to the defenceless, before those who faced him without flinching he cringed like the coward he was. Lording it over the abject, to real force of character he bowed in all submission. An enemy in arms he would meet with blandishments, but crushed with brutal severity a beaten foe. In the former he inspired no fear, with the latter he kept no faith. A trickster, a flatterer, and a craven; a slave, moreover, to wine and venery. Greedy of gold, as he was, and a seeker after court favour, it is hard to say whether avarice or servility predominated in his soul.

(In 1177 John de Courci ventured on an expedition into Ulster on his own account: it was the first time an English force had penetrated into that province. After marching for three days through Meath and Uriel,‡ on the fourth day [*Feb. 1st*] he reached Down, the capital of Ulidia,§ and not being expected by the natives entered the city with little opposition [*Gerald says without any*]. The country, however, soon armed against him,

---

* Ovid, *Amores*, I. viii. 104 (Gerald's quotation is not verbatim.)

† Ps. lv. 21.

‡ Uriel, or Oriel, comprised the later counties of Louth, Armagh, Monaghan and most of Fermanagh. It thus stretched across Ireland from sea to sea, and formed the southern border of Ulster.

§ Down and Antrim.

and five battles were fought, the first two and the last of which he won. The mixed races of north Ireland seem to have fought better than their Kelt-Iberian fellow-countrymen of the south, for they beat the invaders twice, and this is noted by Gerald in connection with the campaign and again below * [*chap.* 20]. In the Irish hero-tales Ulster is always more than a match for the rest of Ireland.)

A.D. 1177.—[Concerning the invasion of Ulster by John de Courci and the doings of Vivianus the legate.]

Wilelm. Newburg. Hist. Rer. Anglic. 1177.

John de Courci, getting together a strong body of horse and foot, conceived the idea of invading that province of Ireland which is separated from the kingdom of Scotland by a narrow strait and is named Ulster. There had chanced to come from Scotland thither, as legate of the Apostolic See, one Vivianus, a man of great eloquence; he had been respectfully received by the king and bishops of the province, and was staying for the time being in the maritime state called Down. Now when the approach of the enemy was reported, the Irish consulted the legate as to what should be done at such a crisis. He replied that they should fight for their fatherland, and on their deciding to do so gave them his benediction and offered up prayers for their success. Animated by this they rushed boldly to battle, but were easily overcome and put to flight by the mail-clad cavalry and the archers of the English. In consequence of

* Connaught, which practically maintained its independence, was Keltic; but it had great geographical advantages.

this defeat the city of Down fell into the hands of the victors. Then the Roman legate took refuge with his attendants in a church which was renowned for the relics of saints. But he was a prudent man, and had provided himself with letters from the king of the English to his officials in Ireland, to the end that backed by their good-will he might carry out the duties of his legation among the barbarians. Protected by the authority of these credentials, he passed on to Dublin, and, acting confidently in the name either of his lord the pope or of the king of the English, called together the bishops and abbots of the island and proclaimed a general council [*March* 13*th*, 1177]. But on his proposing with too much precipitancy to introduce the Romish discipline into the simple native church, he received notice from the royal officers to depart out of the country or to lend his support to their arms; whereupon he returned to Scotland, laden with less of the longed-for Irish gold than he had hoped to carry off with him. John de Courci and his followers had now occupied the adjacent territory of Downpatrick as well as the town itself, and, after repelling the attacks of the Irish princes, went on to take Armagh by storm. This is considered the metropolitan city of Ireland, out of reverence for St. Patrick and other saints of the land whose sacred relics are deposited there. He thus subdued the whole district. The people of this province [*Ulster*] are said to have been until that time superstitious beyond all the Irish tribes in the matter of the celebration of Easter. For, as I have been told by a

G

certain venerable bishop of that race, they think they are doing service to God in accumulating through the year by theft and rapine goods to be wastefully consumed during the Paschal solemnities in providing most extravagant banquets, in honour, forsooth, of our Lord. And there used to be great rivalry among them lest haply any one should be surpassed by his fellows in the lavish preparation of viands and dishes. But this most superstitious custom they relinquished together with their liberty when conquered.

(We may notice here in passing a complete change of front in the policy of Vivianus, who at the synod he convoked at Dublin enjoined submission to the English king under pain of excommunication. See, too, a note on Gerald, II. 19, below.)

A.D. 1177.—[Victory of de Courci at Downpatrick.]

Annals of Innisfallen: 1177 ; *O'Donovan's Translation from the Irish.*

" Melaghlin O'Neill, at the head of the Kinel-Owen [*men of Keneleonia*], and Rory [*Roderic*] Mac Donlevy, at the head of the Ulidians, accompanied by the archbishop of Armagh, . . . the bishop of Ulidia [*Down*], and the clergy of the north of Ireland, repaired with their noble relics * to Downpatrick, to take it from John de Courci. A fierce battle was fought between them, in which the Kinel-Owen and Ulidians were defeated, with the loss of 500 men.

* Cp. the sacred host and the banners of the saints in the English army at the battle of the Standard in 1138, and the " carroccio" of the Italian republics.

... The archbishop of Armagh, the bishop of Down, and all the clergy were taken prisoners; and the English got possession of the crosiers of St. Comgall * and St. Dachiarog,† the Book of Armagh,‡ besides a Bell called Ceolan an 'Tighearna [*musical bell of the Kings*]. They afterwards, however, set the bishops at liberty, and restored the Book of Armagh and the Bell, but they killed all the inferior clergy, and kept the other noble relics, which . . . are still in the hands of the English."

A description of John de Courci.

Girald. Cambr. Expug. Hibern. Lib. II. cap. xviii.

John de Courci was a tall, fair man, with big-boned, muscular limbs, large of frame and powerfully built. He had great personal strength, and his intrepidity was remarkable. A born soldier, in action he was always to be found in the van taking upon himself the brunt of the battle. Such was his impatience and his eagerness for the fray, that, even when in command, he would usually forget that a general should be calm and self-possessed: the leader became lost in the soldier. With headlong impetuosity he habitually flew to the front, so that there was a risk that if his men

---

* Flourished *circa* 550. His saint's day is May 10th. "Every Sunday he used to eat" (*Martyrology of Donegal*).

† Prophet, and patron saint of Errigal-Keeroge in Tyrone: commemorated on May 7th.

‡ Written about the beginning of the ninth century. It contained the New Testament, the canon of St. Patrick, a sketch of his life, etc. This MS., which is on vellum and written in Old Irish and Latin, is still in existence.

wavered in their support of him, victory would be lost through his seeking it with too much haste. Yet although in the excitement of a fight he knew no restraint and acted more like an ordinary man-at-arms than a commander, in private life he was a discreet and sober-minded man; one, moreover, who yielded proper reverence to the Church of Christ. For he was at all times a regular attendant at divine worship, and showed by public thanksgiving that he ascribed to the heavenly grace any success that he attained. Did he achieve a deed of glory, the glory of that deed he recognized as due to God. But since, as Tully says, 'No one thing has Nature elaborated to absolute perfection in every point,'* the blemishes of extreme parsimony and inconstancy stained the snowy whiteness of the many virtues I have mentioned.

He married a daughter of Guthred, king of Man, and after a long and severe struggle, in which the fortune of war shifted now to this side, now to that, he at length firmly established himself as the conqueror and kept the country under by building castles in advantageous positions throughout the whole of Ulster. Thus he finally restored peace and settled order, though only after undergoing much toil and privation and many dangers.

It strikes me, by the way, as a remarkable fact that these four main pillars of the Irish conquest, Fitz-Stephen, Hervey, Reimund, and John de Courci, by some mysterious though doubtless equitable ordinance of the Almighty, were not deemed deserving of the

* Cic. *Inv.* ii. 3.

blessing of lawful issue by their wives. I might add to these a fifth, namely, Meiler, whose wife up to the present time has borne him no offspring.

A.D. 1177.—Invasion of Connaught.
Girald. Cambr. Expug. Hibern. Lib. II. cap. xix.

After this,* Milo de Cogan, who under Fitz-Aldelm was Constable of the garrison of Dublin, and had for the second time been appointed Warden of the City, with 40 men-at-arms—20 of whom were led by Ralph, a son of Fitz-Stephen, and a youth of great promise—, 200 mounted retainers and 300 bowmen, crossed the Shannon and boldly invaded Connaught, which hitherto had not been attacked by the English. Then the men of Connaught with their own hands set fire to their towns and villages in all directions. They burnt, too, their churches, and whatever provisions could not be hidden in the crypts.† Finally, in order to bring scandal upon our people and to call forth the divine vengeance upon their heads, they took down the crucifixes and the images of the saints and

---

* The synod at Dublin.

† As in England during the Danish invasions treasures were often concealed in the crypts of the monasteries, so in Ireland in troublous times provisions were carried to the churches for safe keeping. The legate Vivianus had ordered that the English troops were to have the right of buying such stores on due payment [Gerald, II. 19]. The buildings were burnt that they might not be used as quarters by the English. The Irish houses, and usually even the churches, were built of wood and wattle-work; hence the need for and use of the Round Towers.

strewed them over the plains in the path of our advancing forces. The English troops penetrated as far as Tuam, which is the chief city of those parts, and made a stay of eight days in the land of the enemy; but finding the country stripped of supplies, they then fell back upon the Shannon. There they found Roderic, king of Connaught, posted in a wood near the river, with his host in three large divisions. A fierce engagement ensued, but de Courci, after making much slaughter among the Irishry, got off with the loss of only three archers, and retreated to Dublin.*

(This same year, 1177, Fitz-Aldelm was recalled together with Milo de Cogan and Fitz-Stephen, and Hugh de Laci was sent out as procurator, while Fitz-Aldelm returned as 'dapifer' and governor of Wexford, and Milo de Cogan and Fitz-Stephen as joint governors of Desmond, Robert le Poer being appointed 'marescallus' and governor of Waterford. Fitz-Aldelm, according to Gerald [who, however, is no friend to him, as his 'descriptio' shows] had not distinguished himself in any way during his procuratorship.)

A description of [Robert] Fitz-Stephen.

Girald. Cambr. Expug. Hibern. Lib. I. cap. xxvi.

O gallant soul, matchless example of heroism and true enterprise! O thou sport of fickle destiny, now and again prosperous, but far more often not!

* In the "Four Masters" it is stated that this invasion was prompted by Murrough, son of Roderic, and that the former was afterwards punished, his father ordering his eyes to be put out. In early times blindness was for all political purposes equivalent to death.

Gallant, indeed, who both in Ireland and in Wales bore with unruffled spirit many a vicissitude of fate !

> With weal or woe inconstant Fortune toyed,
> By turns he suffered, and by turns enjoyed.*

Verily, Fitz-Stephen, thou wert a second Marius! For consider the Roman or thyself in the hour of success, and marvel that success could be so brilliant : look at thyself or him in adversity, how profound that adversity !

Fitz-Stephen was a well-favoured man of burly make, and sound and vigorous health ; in stature slightly above the middle height. A free liver and open-handed, he had a hearty way with him : in short was a right good fellow, but given over-much to wine and women.

A.D. 1178.—[The two defeats of de Courci in Ulster.]

Annals of the Four Masters: 1178 ; *O'Donovan's Translation from the Irish.*

"John de Courci with his foreigners repaired to Machaire Conaille [*in the level part of co. Louth*], and committed depredations there. They encamped for a night [*by the bridge of Newry*] in Glenree [" *The Vale of the river Righe*"], where Murrough O'Carroll, lord of Uriel, and Cooley MacDonlevy, king of Ulidia, made a hostile attack upon them, and drowned and otherwise killed 450 of them. 100 of the Irish, together with O'Hanvy, lord of Hy-Meith-Macha [*in co. Monaghan*], fell in the heat of the battle.

* Luc. *Pharsal.* II. 131.

John de Courci soon after proceeded to plunder Dalaradia [*co. Down*] and Hy-Tuirtre [*in Ulidia*], and Cumee O'Flynn, lord of Hy-Tuirtre and Firlee [*in co. Antrim*], gave battle to him and his foreigners and defeated them with great slaughter, through the miracles of Patrick, Columbkille, and Brendan;* and John himself escaped with difficulty, being severely wounded, and fled to Dublin.

The Constable of the king of England in Dublin and East Meath (namely Hugo) † marched with his forces to Clonmacnoise [*in King's Co.*] and plundered all the town except the churches and the bishop's houses. God and Kieran ‡ wrought a manifest miracle against them, for they were unable to rest or sleep, until they had secretly absconded from Cuirr Cluana on the next day.

The river Galway was dried up for a period of a natural day; all the articles that had been lost in it from remotest times, as well as its fish, were collected by the inhabitants of the fortress, and by the people of the country in general."

* St. Brendan, or Brandan, abbot of Clonfert, was the great sailor-saint. He died in 576, the year before the battle of Dyrham, and his death day and saint's day is May 16th.

"Seven years on a whale's back he spent,
"It was a difficult mode of piety."
(*Martyrology of Donegall*).

† Hugh de Laci.

‡ St. Kieran, founder and first abbot of the monastery of Clonmacnoise, died September 9th, 549. The day of his death is his saint's day. He died, then, just when the Angles were beginning to found the kingdom of Northumbria.

(From the 5th to the 19th of March, 1179, there sat, under the presidency of pope Alexander iii, the famous "Concilium Lateranense," the eleventh *general* council [but first general council of Lateran], to discuss matters of ecclesiastical discipline. As representatives of the Irish Church went Laurence O'Toole archbishop of Dublin, Catholicus archbishop of Tuam, and five or six bishops).

Benedict. Abbat. Gest. reg. Hen. II.: 1178.

And they [*the above prelates*] swore to the king on the Holy Gospels that they designed nothing to the prejudice of the crown or kingdom of England.

A.D. 1182.—[Assassination of Milo de Cogan: Irish account.]

Annals of Loch Cé: 1182; *Hennessy's Translation from the Irish.*

"Milo de Cogan, after assuming the kingship of Cork and Desmond, and after plundering Ath-cliath [*Dublin*], and Port-Lairge [*Waterford*], and Cork; and after destroying all Erinn, both church and territory, was slain by Mac Tire, king of Ui-Mac-caille [*in co. Cork*], and [there was] a slaughter of foreigners along with him, (viz.) :—Mac Sleimme, and Thomas Sugach ("Thomas the Merry"), and Cenn-cuilinn (Reimund of Kantitune?), and Remunn (Reimund Fitz-Hugh), and two sons of [Fitz-]Stephen, and a great many more."

A.D. 1182.—Assassination of Milo de Cogan [English account].

Girald. Cambr. Expug. Hibern. Lib. II. cap. xx.

Fitz-Stephen and Milo de Cogan had now jointly governed Desmond in peace for five years, curbing by the example of their moderation the impetuosity of the younger men both among their own followers and among the natives, when Milo and Ralph, a son of Fitz-Stephen * and lately married to Milo's daughter, set out for Lismore. While sitting in a field awaiting a conference with the men of Waterford, they were suddenly attacked and murdered with axe-blows from behind by five men headed by the traitor Mac Tire, who was to have been their host that night. The opportunity suggested by this calamity at once disturbed the whole country to such an extent that Dermot Mac Carthy, and with him almost all the Irish of that region, threw off their allegiance to the English and rose in revolt against Fitz-Stephen, who had already so often experienced the mutability of fortune. Nor did the district afterwards revert to its former tranquillity until Reimund succeeded as heir to his uncle Fitz-Stephen and obtained the sole custody of the city ; † and perhaps not even then.

As it is with all other nations, in the North of Ireland the inhabitants are warlike, while those of the southern parts are crafty. The one people seekers after fame, the other seekers after fraud; the former

* See Gerald, Bk. II. chap. 19 just above.
† Cork.

rest their hopes on war, the latter on their wiles; those put forth their strength, these descend to stratagem; there we find battle, here betrayal. Pertinent to this are the words of the poet:—

> Braced by the breezes of the Northern spring,
> The warrior comes who knoweth not dismay;
> No fears hath hideous death for him, no sting;
> Nor yieldeth he, nor wavereth in the fray.
>
> But he who droops in burning Southern vales,
> Where hot-breathed zephyrs enervate the frame,
> Unused to toil, where tilth no toil entails,
> Feeble in arms, at coward arts will aim.

* * * * *

Very soon after we find a worthy successor to the energetic Milo de Cogan in the person of his brother Richard,* who had been sent to fill the place of the former by command of the king of the English, and with him there went a body of picked knights.

When the greater part of the winter had passed, at the end of February [1183], a nephew of Fitz-Stephen, Philip de Barri, an upright and judicious man, sailed over to Ireland with a strong force. He came with the twofold object of helping his uncle, and of guarding his rights over Olethan,† a territory granted to him by Fitz-Stephen, but of which he had been wrongfully deprived by his cousin Ralph.‡

There came, too, in the same vessel another

---

* See Gerald, I. 21. above.
† South-east part of the modern county of Cork.
‡ Mentioned above in this chapter.

nephew of Fitz-Stephen, a brother of Philip, who by his advice gave great assistance to both his uncle and his brother, and besides was at great pains to investigate the topography, the natural history, and the race-lore of the island. For he was a diligent student of letters, and his name stands upon the title-page of this book.*

It was about this time that Hervey de Montmaurice retired from the world and became a monk in the famous monastery of the Holy Trinity at Canterbury. He had previously endowed that house with the churches on his lands along the coast between Waterford and Wexford. Would that with the cowl he had assumed a Christian spirit! Would that with his military career he had laid aside his malice!

A.D. 1177.—How peace and order were established in the realm of Ireland by Hugh de Laci.

Girald. Cambr. Expug. Hibern. Lib. II. cap. xxi.

To return, however: while these things were going on in Desmond, Hugh de Laci, who was a man of great activity, integrity and discretion, had secured Leinster and Meath by building castles in situations well chosen for commanding the country. Among others he erected in a position naturally strong the castle of Leighlin overlooking the noble river Barrow, on the Ossory side of the stream, in Odrone.† This

* Giraldus Cambrensis himself.
† Odrone or Idrone was a district in the modern county of Carlow.

border post had been held by Robert le Poer, but he was withdrawn by the king's command.

A pretty pair of lords marchers these fellows Robert le Poer [*le Pauvre*] and Fitz-Aldelm were to be sent to a land which wanted men of dignity and valour to defend it!

> So doth a freak of fate, amazing all,
> Some low-born carl to giddy greatness haul.*

They were warriors—

> Who loved to loll in lady's bower,
> And to twang the guitar by the lazy hour;
> But shrank from the notion of war's alarms,
> From the shield that would tire their delicate arms;
> Then the terrible lance! And their tears would gush
> At the thought how a helmet their curls would crush;

Such were the bold lords marchers whom the king had placed in power.

Indeed it is a wonder that so magnificent and vigorous a prince should, simply for personal reasons, have appointed to the wardenships of far-distant borders men so unlike himself, mere degraded and spiritless parasites of his court.

But Hugh de Laci, who was none of this sort, made it his first care to peacefully reinstate the natives who after having submitted to the above-mentioned knaves, had been violently ejected by them from their territory. To these he restored the pastures which had been lying deserted by their herds, and the fields which had been robbed of their cultivators. Having by his clemency and strict adherence to agreements

* Juv. iii. 39.

won the confidence and good-will of the Irish in the country parts, he next by degrees got the townsfolk everywhere under control, and compelled them to submit to his rule and obey the laws. In this way he brought about that the ruin and disorganization caused by his predecessors was reduced to order; and where others had reaped only toil and trouble, he was the first to realize satisfactory results. In fine, before long he had established such peace in the land, had so bountifully enriched all his adherents at the expense of his opponents, so gained the hearts of the natives by his liberal treatment of them and by his affability, while he allied himself personally with their chiefs, as to give rise to a strong suspicion that he had it in his mind to throw off his allegiance and seize for himself the royal dignity.

[Grant of land by Hugh de Laci to William the Little.]

Translated from the vellum MS. in the Clarendon Collection.

[*Labelled*] A genuine copy of an ancient charter granted by Hugh de Laci to William the Little.

Hugh de Laci to all sons of Holy Mother Church and to his liegemen and friends, French and English and Irish, greeting. Know ye that I have given and granted, and by the present charter confirmed to William the Little and to his heirs Matherothirnan with all its purtenances, except the lake and vill which is called Dissert [*Dysart*] and one knight's fee around the aforesaid town which I retain in my own hands,

except also two vills, to wit, Rauakonnil and Clonra—
[*obliterated*], which I have before given to Adam de
Totipon [*sic*], and except half of the wood which is
between Rauakonnil and Killar, of which wood the
moiety that is nearest to Rauakonnil I have before
given to the aforesaid Adam. [I grant] besides to
the aforesaid William the Little and to his heirs as an
addition two lands which do not belong to the aforesaid land, to wit, Levelkeil and Kleonkelli, together
with the aforesaid land: to be had and held in fee
and in inheritance of me and of my heirs freely and
undisturbed, honourably and fully, in churches and
chapels, in wood and plain, in meadows and pastures,
in ways and byways, in waters and fisheries, in ponds
and mills and hunting grounds, with all liberties and
free customs thence arising for the service of one
knight [*obliterated*] thirty carucates * of the aforesaid
land. Given at Killar. These witnesses: Robert de
Hautvilliers; Gilbert de Nugent; Robert de Bigarz;
Simon de Bigarz; Meiler Fitz-Henry; Thomas Fitz-Alfred; Nicholas de Dinon; John de Eustreville;
William de Fuone, priest; Nicholas de Vico; Radulf,
clerk; Philip, clerk.†

A description of Hugh de Laci.

Girald. Cambr. Expug. Hibern. Lib. II. cap. xxii.

If you wish to know what Hugh de Laci was like,
picture to yourself a swarthy man with small, black,

* A carucate was one hundred acres.

† This barony of Petit is in West Meath, and the Petits
became barons of Mullingar.

deeply-sunken eyes, a flat nose, and his right cheek disfigured down to the chin by an ugly scar caused by some accidental burn: a man with a short neck and a hairy and muscular body, though small and ill-made. With all this, however, he had considerable strength of character and resolution, and for temperance was a very Frenchman. He was a careful man in his private affairs, and when in office most vigilant in the discharge of public business. Although he had had much experience in military matters, still he was not fortunate as a general, and in his campaigns frequently sustained reverses. After the death of his wife, he fell into habits of lax morality. His fondness for money amounted to avarice; but he was also ambitious beyond measure of honour and renown.

A.D. 1181.—The coming of John the constable and Richard de Pec.

Girald. Cambr. Expug. Hibern. Lib. II. cap. xxiii.

In this condition of things, and when the above suspicions were continually being intensified by report, there came into the island about the 1st of May John, Constable of Chester, and Richard de Pec, who had been sent across by the king of the English to recall Hugh and to take over the government as joint commissioners.* But before Hugh left they all consulted

* Howden is silent about these suspicions, and gives as the reason for Laci's recall that he had married the daughter of the king of Connaught without Henry's consent [which, however, would in itself be a suspicious step], and according to the usage

together and built a large number of castles throughout Leinster; for till that time there had been plenty in Meath, but too few in the former province.

* * * * *

This castle-building was carried out during the summer, and in the following winter John and Richard were recalled to England, and Hugh, who had allayed the royal suspicions, returned again to his charge. But a certain clerk, one Robert of Shrewsbury, was associated with him on the king's behalf, to act as his coadjutor and adviser, and to keep an eye on his doings. Hugh, on his arrival, set himself again to building more castles.

A.D. 1180.—Death of Laurence, archbishop of Dublin, at Eu, and succession of John Comyn.

Girald. Cambr. Expug. Hibern. Lib. II. cap. xxiv.

Meanwhile Laurence, archbishop of Dublin, had died at Eu, a town of Normandy, on Friday, November 14th,* 1180. He was a good and just man, but,

of that country, which may refer to the Irish custom of marriage on trial for one year from the feast of Samhain (*Allhallows*) to the feast of Samhain. *Cf.* Book of Rights, edited by O'Donovan, p. 243; Campion, Historie of Ireland, p. 23; Irish Nennius, pp. 179, 182.

* Laurence O'Toole, archbishop of Dublin, 1162–1180, was canonized, the day of his death, November 14th, being his saint's day. The chief points to note concerning him in connection with England and the English conquest of Ireland are (1) His mediating at Dublin in 1170 between Dermot and the Ostmen, probably because he regarded Dermot as lawful over-king of the

through zeal for his nation, as it is said, had asserted when present at the Lateran council certain ecclesiastical privileges which are opposed to the royal dignity. For this reason he had fallen under the king's displeasure, and had been detained ever since either in England or across the sea in France. At Eu, however, he found a happy end to a life which exile had rendered burdensome. In connection with him, among various miracles which God—manifesting His wonders even in our days—wrought in the person of this His saint, the following marvel that occurred in those parts stands out conspicuous above the rest. When this holy man was seized at Abbeville with mortal sickness, he refused to listen to the advice of his attendants that he should remain where he was, for he said that his place was not there. But passing thence towards the town of Eu, as soon as he caught sight of the cathedral of St. Mary, and heard that it was dedicated to the blessed Virgin, he prophetically quoted the verse that says " This is my resting-place for ever: Here will I dwell; for I have desired it." *

Norse settlers in the city; for since the battle of Clontarf in 1014 the Ostmen had admitted the supremacy of the Irish princes. (2) His joining the native league of 1171 under Roderic of Connaught, which besieged the earl in Dublin. (3) His submission to Henry in 1171 or 1172 with the other prelates at the synod of Cashel. The reasons for this were probably *a*. Resistance appeared hopeless. *b*. There seemed a chance of some reform of public morality. *c*. There was a prospect of the advancement of the Church of Ireland. (4) His attitude in 1179 at the Lateran council, which offended the English king, as related in this chapter.

* Ps. 132. 14.

SUCCESSION OF ARCHBISHOP JOHN.

And in that very town within a few days was he released from human cares, and buried with due solemnities in its cathedral. Nor did the Lord suffer his light to be hid, but also proclaimed him by working many potent signs and prodigies at his tomb.

He was succeeded by John Comyn, an Englishman by nationality,* who through the royal influence was elected at Evesham in England by the clergy of Dublin with sufficient unanimity and concord.† By the Roman pontiff Lucius he was at Veletri ordained a cardinal priest ‡ and consecrated an archbishop. He was a learned and eloquent man, who by his zeal in the cause of justice and his appreciation of what was due to the exalted office to which he had been raised, would have greatly improved the position and condition of the Irish Church, had not the crosier been ever held in check by the sword, the priesthood by the kingly power, virtue by jealousy. For even as the flesh is opposed to the spirit, so are carnal men opposed to those who are spiritual; so do the servants of Cæsar strive with unending malice against the soldiers of Christ.

* His family held lands in Scotland.

† Hoveden does not mention any election by the clergy of Dublin, and it is difficult to see how they could have elected him at Evesham. Perhaps Gerald means that a notification of his election was sent to him there, or that a deputation from the Dublin clergy met him at that place on his way to Ireland.

‡ There is no other authority for this statement. The pope was Lucius III. [1181–5], who succeeded Alexander III.

A.D. 1184.—The sending of John, archbishop of Dublin, into Ireland.

Girald. Cambr. Expug. Hibern. Lib. II. cap. xxv.

The king of the English now determined to carry into effect a design which he had long entertained, namely the transferring of the lordship of all Ireland to his youngest son John, who, with his father's assent, had shortly before received the homage of the people of that land. He, therefore, about the 1st of August, despatched John, archbishop of Dublin, as precursor, to arrange for the coming of the prince. Forthwith Hugh de Laci was recalled, and about the 1st of September Philip of Worcester, a sumptuous and liberal man but a good soldier, was sent over as procurator in his stead with 40 men-at-arms.*

A.D. 1185.—The coming into Ireland of John, the king's son.

Rob^{tus} de Monte.

[John], whom men call 'Lackland,' though he has broad possessions of his own and swarms of retainers, crossed over to Ireland, the grace of God permitting him to be king in that country.

Girald. Cambr. Expug. Hibern. Lib. II. cap. xxxii.

When all that was wanted for so important an expedition had by his father's care been provided and

---

* Hugh de Laci disregarded the royal commands and remained in Ireland (*see below sub anno* 1186).

prepared, in the following Lent, John, the English king's youngest son, on whom had been conferred the government of Ireland, travelled along the coast-road of South Wales * and arrived at Pembroke. He was accompanied throughout his journey up to the point of embarkation by that eminent man Ralph de Glanville, then chief privy councillor of the king and Justiciar of all England. On the fourth day of Passover [*Wednesday, April 24th*], the wished-for east wind came, and the prince went on board the noble fleet which was lying in Milford Haven. But as the suitable breeze had sprung up sooner than was expected, John had omitted to pay his visit to the venerable cathedral of St. David. This was an unlucky omen.†

At eventide they stood out to sea, and the passage was made by about noon the next day, when they put in at Waterford and there landed, to the number of some 300 men-at-arms and many mounted retainers and archers.

Then were again fulfilled the prophecies of Merlin the Wild which were applied above to the prince's father.‡ To these he adds touching the son :—

> Born of the fell fire-king, a sparklet prince shall dart
> His bolt of icy fear to Erin's quaking heart.

Prince John thus landed in Ireland in the 22nd year of his age, in the 13th year from the invasion of

* See above Gerald, Bk. I. chaps. 16 and 28.
† His father had not forgotten in 1171 to pay his devotions at St. David's, and to commend his Irish "crusade" to Heaven.
‡ See above Gerald, Bk. I. chap. 30.

his father, the 14th from that of the earl, the 15th from that of Fitz-Stephen,* and in the year 1185 from the incarnation of our Lord: Lucius [III.] the successor of Alexander III. being pope, Frederic [I.] emperor, and Philip [II.] son of Lewis [VII.] king of France.

Several ecclesiastics went over in the same ship with the prince, one of whom had been specially sent by the king to attend him. This man was a diligent enquirer into natural history, and having spent in all two years in the island—reckoning both visits together—brought back with him as the worthy reward of his labours the materials for his *Prophetic History* † and his *Topography*.‡ Afterwards, when in Brittany, he devoted such time as he could spare from his duties at court to carefully digesting and arranging these notes. This took five years, three of which were occupied in the composition of the *Topography*, two were given to the *Prophetic History:* works which though they are looked at askance by men to-day, will assuredly be read by posterity; though carped at by the former, will afford pleasure to the latter; regarded with despite as they are now, will be valued in the ages yet to come.

* The figures are not correct. John was in his nineteenth year, and the succeeding numbers should be fourteen, fifteen, and sixteen respectively.

† The "Expugnatio Hibernica" is often called by Gerald "Vaticinalis Historia."

‡ The "Topographia Hibernica."

A.D. 1185.—Prince John's Dublin charter.

Archives of Dublin.

'John, son of the lord king of England, and lord of Ireland, to his archbishops, bishops, abbots, earls, barons, justices, constables, officers, and all his bailiffs and liegemen, French, English, and Irish greeting :

Know ye that I have conceded and by my present charter confirmed to my men of Bristol the grant which the lord king of England, my father, made to them : to wit my city of Dublin to dwell in.

Wherefore I will, and steadfastly enjoin, that they have and hold it of me and of my heirs, well and in peace, freely and undisturbed, entirely and fully and honourably, with all liberties and free customs which the men of Bristol have in Bristol and throughout all the land of the lord king of England, my father, as his charter witnesseth.

Witnesses: Hugh de Laci, constable ; Bertram de Verdun, my seneschal; Gilbert Pipard ; William de Wennecy, steward ; Alard, my chamberlain ; Adam de Hereford ; Philip de Worcester ; Robert de Mortemer. At Kildare.

A.D. 1185.—"John grants to the canons of St. Thomas of Dublin the tenth of ale which he has by usage from the taverns of Dublin and also his custom of ale and metheglin" [*mead-liquor*].

Archives of Dublin.

I. John, son of the lord king of England, and lord of Ireland, to his bailiffs of Ireland greeting :

Know ye that I have given unto God and the canons of St. Thomas of Dublin the tenth of ale which I have by usage from the taverns of Dublin for the maintenance of the same canons, and therefore steadfastly enjoin that they have and hold it well and in peace.

Witness: brother Richard, my almoner.* At Windsor.

II. John, son of the king of England, and lord of Ireland, to his archbishops, bishops, abbots, earls, barons, justices, constables, and all his bailiffs throughout Ireland greeting:

Know ye that I, for the salvation of my soul and the souls of my ancestors, have given and granted and by this my present charter confirmed to God and to the church of St. Thomas at Dublin, and to the canons serving the same house, in free and perpetual alms † for ever the customs of ale and mead which I have been accustomed to have in the taverns of Dublin.

Wherefore I will and steadfastly enjoin that the aforesaid church and the aforesaid canons have and hold the aforesaid custom from the aforesaid taverns, well and in peace, freely and undisturbed, entirely and fully and honourably, with all the purtenances thereof, as ever I fullest held the same.

Witnesses: John Marshal; William Marshal; Bertram de Verdun; Gilbert Pipard; Galfrid de Constentin; Roger de Ilanes; and Alexander Arsic.

* A Templar.   † Frankalmoigne.

A.D. 1185.—[Irish account of the administration of prince John.]

Annals of the Four Masters: 1185; *O'Donovan's Translation from the Irish.*

"The son of the king of England, that is, John, the son of Henry II., came to Ireland with a fleet of 60 ships, to assume the government of the kingdom. He took possession of Dublin and Leinster, and erected castles at Tipraid Fachtna [*in S. W. Kilkenny*] and Ardfinan [*in Tipperary*], out of which he plundered Munster; but his people were defeated with great slaughter by Donnell O'Brien [*king of Thomond*]. The son of the king of England then returned to England * to complain to his father of Hugh de Laci, who was the king of England's deputy in Ireland on his (*John's*) arrival, and who had prevented the Irish kings from sending him (*John*) either tribute or hostages."

A.D. 1185.—[The ill government of prince John.]

Benedict. Abbat. Gest. reg. Hen. II.: 1185.

But prince John himself met with scant success; partly because of the defection of those natives who ought to have held loyally to him, but especially because he would not pay his hired knights and soldiers. In the repeated conflicts which occurred between his followers and the Irishry, the royal army

---

* As prince John was superseded by John de Courci in September 1185, his rule in Ireland lasted only five months, and he returned to England in the following December.

fell almost entirely to pieces. For most of the cavalry and footmen who had come over with him deserted, and arrayed themselves on the side of the natives against him. And so it happened that the aforesaid John, the king's son, owing to his greed, found himself without support and had to leave Ireland and return to England.

Of the credit due to Fitz-Stephen, the earl, and the king, and how far they may be acquitted of certain charges.

Girald. Cambr. Expug. Hibern. Lib. II. cap. xxxiii.

We have seen that Fitz-Stephen led the way and opened a path for the earl, the earl for the king, the king for his son John. Much credit, therefore, is due to him who had the enterprise and the hardihood to set the first precedent. Much, too, to him who as it were formed the connecting link, and lent an additional impulse to the undertaking so gallantly begun. Yet far more praise still must we yield to him who added the weight of his great authority in order to complete and consummate the conquest.

Here I must call attention to the fact that Fitz-Stephen and the earl, both of whom aided in the just restoration of Dermot, the one on terms of vassalage, the other as being allied to him by marriage with his daughter, founded their position on his grants, and therefore are clearly not mere freebooters so far as Leinster is concerned. As for the case of Waterford, however, and those parts of Desmond and Meath which the earl seized in so high-handed a manner, I have no excuse to offer. Now the lordship over the fifth part of the island, which was unquestionably the earl's in right of his wife, he transferred in full to the king of the English; while the rest of the Irish princes by spontaneously and without delay offering themselves as vassals to the king, gave the latter an indubitable supremacy over the whole of Ireland. Wherefore, to say nothing of the arguments, new or old, which have been previously adduced in support of this claim, from the above considerations alone it is absolutely plain that the English entered the country by no means so unjustly as some ignorant persons imagine.*

Of the lets and delays to the full and perfect conquest of Ireland.

Girald. Cambr. Expug. Hibern. Lib. II. cap. xxxiv.

Happy would this island have been, long since would it have been vigorously and successfully subdued from end to end, long since reduced without difficulty to systematic order and kept well in hand by the building of castles from sea to sea in commanding situations on every side, had it not been for the royal edict which cut off the supplies of the first invaders; or rather, perhaps I should say if domestic plots † had not so prematurely recalled the king from

* In the Annals of Loch Cé, *sub anno* 1170, the adventurers are called pirates.
† The rebellion in 1173 of the king's sons, abetted by the queen.

that proud and noble expedition which he conducted himself in person.

Happy, too, if the worth of the original conquerors had been only appreciated as it deserved, and the care and conduct of the government been committed to the strong hands of those brave and trusty men.

For the natives of the land at our first coming had been astounded and thrown into consternation by the startling novelty of the event, and were terrified at the speed with which the archers shot and at the might of the heavy men-at-arms. But delay—which ever brings danger in its train—, the protracted, dilatory, and feeble character of the conquest, and the unskilfulness and cowardice of procurators and governors who only lulled their own side into a false security, all combined to give them heart. Moreover, by gradual and careful training in the use of the bow and other weapons, by learning caution and studying the art of ambuscade, by the confidence gained from frequently engaging in conflict with our troops, lastly taught by our very successes, these Irishmen whom at first we could rout with ease, became able to offer a stout resistance.

Read the Book of the Kings, read the Prophets, go through the whole of the Old Testament; consider, too, the familiar examples of our own times, our own country; never will you find an instance of a nation being conquered except in punishment for its sins. Either, then, the Irish race, which for its crimes and vices had deserved to be chastised by foreign invasion, had still not yet so irretrievably offended the Supreme Judge as to merit entire destruction or subjection: or the English people had not yet by reason of their virtues been deemed worthy of obtaining full power and peaceful mastery over the nation that they had partially vanquished and subdued. Therefore, neither having altogether forfeited or altogether earned the favour of Heaven, perchance it was the Divine vengeance which kept both so long in a state of war, in such a way that the one has never yet quite reached the pinnacle of victory, the other has never quite bowed the neck to the yoke of servitude.

The Irish have four prophets, Moling, Berchan,* Patrick, and Columba,† whose writings are in Irish and still extant among them. They speak of this conquest, and all pronounce that it will be terrible, entailing many battles, a long struggle, and much bloodshed, which will continue into the times of far-distant generations. Indeed, they hardly allow that complete victory will be attained by the English, and the island be entirely subjugated from sea to sea and planted with castles, before the Day of Judgment. Berchan, moreover, avers that after the English have experienced reverses there and been weakened by

---

* St. Berchan, circa 690, about contemporary with Bede. Half his life was spent in Alba (Scotland), half in Erin. His saint's day is December 4th. For St. Moling see above *Expug. Hibern.* Lib. I. cap. 16. For St. Patrick see below *Top. Hibern.* Dis. I. cap. 28.

† St. Columba, born 521, died 597, the year of the conversion of Kent His saint's day is June 9th.

defeat, from the solitary mountains of Patrick* an unknown king shall come, who will storm a certain castle in the wooded parts of Ophelan,† and drive almost all of them out of Ireland. These same prophets, however, also assert that England shall always hold the eastern seaboard of the island.

A.D. 1185.—The causes of the untoward events.

Girald. Cambr. Expug. Hibern. Lib. II. cap. xxxvi.

I should say, then, that the prime cause of all was that whereas the king ought in response to the solemn call of the patriarch ‡ to have set out at once in his own person, or might at least with ready devotion and obedience to Christ have sent one of the princes in his stead, he did nothing of the kind. Nay, at the very time of that sacred summons, and while the holy legate was actually present in his court, he despatched this son of his, with an equipment that was more costly than serviceable, not to the East but

---

* Now Croagh-Patrick [St. Patrick's hill] in county Mayo.
† The northern half of the modern county Kildare.
‡ This was Heraclios, patriarch of Jerusalem, who had come backed by a letter from the pope [Lucius iii.] to urge the English king to lead a crusade against the Saracens, for the Latin kingdom of Jerusalem was then threatened by Saladin. Henry, who had little crusading zeal, decided that his duties at home required his presence and attention, and his promise of a donation was not sufficient to soothe the indignant patriarch. During his visit Heraclios, who was accompanied by the grand masters of the Templars and the Knights Hospitallers of St. John as fellow envoys, consecrated the Temple Church and also that of St. John, Clerkenwell.

to the West, not against Saracens but against Christians, thus seeking his own advantage not that of Jesus Christ.

Again, immediately on the landing of the king's son there met him at Waterford the leading natives of those parts, men who had up to that time been loyal and peacefully inclined and who came to welcome him as their lord and receive him with the kiss of peace. But our people who were new to the land and the Normans in the royal train sneezed and laughed at them; and not content with this rudely pulled them by their beards, which they wore long and bushy according to the fashion of their country.* As soon, however, as they made their escape they departed out of the neighbourhood with their families and goods and transferred their allegiance some to the king of the men of Limerick, some to the prince of those of Cork, others to Roderic of Connaught, and laid before them a full account of all they had seen and experienced in connection with the king's son. They said that the prince was a mere boy, surrounded by a troop of striplings like himself; that, as might be expected from his years, his tastes and pursuits were childish, and that judging from their own observations there was no prospect of anything like mature or stable counsels, nor even of tranquillity for Irishmen.

On hearing this report, the three chief pillars of

* The kiss of peace offered by these bearded chieftains, however well meant, was a familiarity which outraged Angevin notions of court etiquette.

Ireland at that time, the kings of Limerick, Connaught, and Cork, who were just about to wait upon the prince in order to tender him their allegiance, bethought themselves that these comparatively petty troubles foreboded greater ones to come. For if insults such as this were offered to trusty and peaceable subjects, what sort of treatment was to be looked for by those like themselves who had proudly asserted their independence by force of arms! They therefore conferred together, and unanimously decided to resist, and to defend with their lives their ancient rights and liberties. The better to carry this determination into effect, a general league was made, and those became friends again who before had been at feud.

I speak from my own knowledge; and to the truth of what I say I can bear witness from personal experience. Inasmuch as we insolently spurned the loyal advances made to us by the natives who met us first, since God at all times shatters the proud, by our conduct on that occasion we deterred not only them but all the chief men of the island from uniting with us in the ties of friendship.

For this people, like all other barbarous races, although they know not what honour is, yet delight beyond measure to be honoured themselves. And though to be convicted of falsehood stirs in them neither fear nor shame, still by their contempt for liars and their respect for honest men, they show that they esteem in others a virtue of which they blush not to find themselves entirely destitute.

What evils can arise from insolence a wise man

may see from the case of Rehoboam the son of Solomon, and taught by the example of another's misfortune, may learn to shun what it is expedient to avoid. For he, following after the counsels of foolish young men, answered his people and said "My little finger is thicker than my father's loins, and if he chastised you with whips, I will chastise you with scorpions."* By this he alienated from him the ten tribes and they adhered to Jeroboam; so a schism was made in the nation, and he lost them for ever.

In addition to the above reasons, the lands of the friendly Irish, who from the first arrival of Fitz-Stephen and the earl had faithfully stood by us, contrary to our promises we took away and gave to new-comers from England; while the ejected natives at once joined our enemies and became hostile spies, guides for them instead of as formerly guides for us, all the more dangerous from our previous intercourse.

The custody, too, of the castles and maritime towns with their adjacent lands, and the control of tribute therefrom which should have been expended for the public good and to the detriment of our adversaries, were entrusted to mere lucre-hunters, who skulked behind their stone walls, gave themselves up to continual drunkenness, and aimlessly squandered and wasted right and left to the ruin of the burghers and the advantage of the foe.

There was this also besides the other mischiefs, that directly the king's son appeared in the land, among a people who were warlike, hostile, rebellious,

* 1 Kings xii. 10 and 11.

and savage, a people in short in no mood to yield obedience, both the civil government and the military command got into the clutches of men who had in their composition more of the thief than the soldier, knights of the carpet rather than knights of the field, rascals intent less on attacking the enemy than on looting the good citizens. Men, I say, and marchers, forsooth, such as Fitz-Aldelm and his like, under whom both Wales and Ireland—since he was governor in each—had to bewail their decay. For they were fellows who neither kept faith with the subdued nor struck the slightest fear into their opponents; strangers to that noble sentiment of higher minds which prompts us 'To spare the humbled and beat down the proud,'* but rather, on the contrary, their way was 'leaving the foe unharmed, the vanquished to despoil.' Whence it happens that nothing has been done to establish a settled state of things in the island, either by making incursions into the hostile districts, by the erection of castles, or by the opening up of the forest-roads—the 'ill ways,' as they are commonly called—for the security of passengers by felling and removing the trees.

The bands of mercenaries followed the example set by their betters, and behaved in the same way as their masters, giving themselves up to wine and women and taking good care to keep inside the towns on the seaboard. Thus the inland parts, which lay nearer to the enemy, and are called march-lands (perhaps Mars' lands, from Mars, would have been a better name for

* Verg. Æn. vi. 853.

them *) were left entirely deserted and unprotected, and the undefended villages and fortified posts situated between the marches and the coast were abandoned to rapine, slaughter and fire. In the growing insolence of the new-comers, the veteran soldiers of the early leaders were slighted and regarded with scant favour; but they kept in the background and held their peace, waiting quietly to see to what all this extravagance and disorder would eventually lead.

In the mean time, however, the state of the island was this:—confusion and misery were rife on every side; not a road was safe; from the axe of the native there was no protection; each day brought us new rumours of disaster to our people. Such was the condition of things in the open country. It was only in the towns that even the semblance of order was preserved, and there all care was drowned in wine, and gold was a full consolation for any blunders or troubles outside the walls.

Over and above this, although at such a crisis, with the storm of war impending, it was high time for military action, certainly no season for legal actions, yet every one was so engrossed in lawsuits, that the old soldiers † were harassed more by their opponents within the fortifications than by the enemy without.

Thus our power was crippled and enfeebled while the boldness and aggression of the enemy increased. Things went on in this way until the new-comers

---

* This, of course, is mere rhetoric; but Gerald can never pass by an opportunity for a pun or a conceit.

† The veterans who had served under the early invaders.

owing to their incompetence—to say nothing of their cowardice—in turn lost credit with the king, who, discerning the merits of the original conquerors and the advantage they had through their long experience of the island, entrusted the administration to John de Courci.* Under him the realm at once began to rejoice in a tranquillity which was complete in proportion as he was superior to his predecessors in courage and warlike energy. For example, he lost no time in marching far inland, even into Cork and Connaught, and gave his troops little opportunity of being corrupted by want of employment, since he never hesitated to risk his fortunes in the ever-doubtful chances of battle, though in so doing he met not always with success, but sometimes with defeat. Would that he had been as much of a leader as a soldier, as heedful a general as he was a doughty knight.

Further, the greatest evil of all is that on the Church of Christ in this new province of ours we bestow nothing, and do not even deem it worthy of such honour as simple gratitude should prompt us to concede; nay more, we actually rob it of its lands and possessions, and strive to curtail or abolish its time-hallowed dignities and ancient privileges.

One night after. I had been pondering more anxiously than usual on all that had happened, especially on the above wrong offered to our Saviour, and many sad reflections had arisen in my mind therefrom, as I slept I saw a vision, perchance the shadow

* In September, 1185.

of my former thoughts. On the morrow I hastened to relate it to John, the venerable archbishop of Dublin, and together we marvelled at it. For I had seemed to see the king's son John; and he was marking out the foundations of a church upon a broad green plain. And when he had traced the outline on the turf, as surveyors do, he went round and compared it with the lines of the original draught to test the exactness of the measurements. He then found that the nave he had planned upon the ground was large enough, but that the chancel was so small as to be wholly out of keeping with the body of the design: as though he had been minded to allot in this island abundant room to the laity, but scant accommodation to the clergy. Then, methought, I pleaded hard, though in vain, that more space should be given to the chancel, more fitting proportions to the church, when, excited, I suppose, by the contention, I suddenly awoke.

Now all these grave disorders, though due in a measure to both causes, still are to be imputed to evil counsels even more than to the tender years of the king's son John. For this, which had always been a rude and savage land, required trained and experienced minds to mould it into shape. To any realm you will, no matter though it may long have enjoyed a healthy state, with a child-king comes woe;* how much the more then if an ignorant and untaught people be committed to an ignorant and untaught stripling prince!

* Eccles. x. 16.

That, however, the serious mischiefs in the land were to be laid at the door of ill government in particular, even the younger sort began to tacitly admit and was considered certain by the older and more discreet. For some men there were who had long held wide possessions in the more fertile parts, either with little foresight granted to them in fee, or even in many cases seized by them with no show of legal right. And it may be that these at times, observing how occupied the sovereign and his advisers were with other matters, had aspirations to the sole dominion of the country; seeing that, when everything was not just as they wished, they appear to have held of light account their allegiance to the king or their loyalty to his son, albeit they were bound to them by fealty, oath, and homage. Threefold though their obligation thus was, they easily found a means and excuse for its violation.

A.D. 1185.—Of the three parties among the invaders at this time.

Girald. Cambr. Expug. Hibern. Lib. II. cap. xxxvii.

To sum up, our men in Ireland fell into three distinct divisions: the Normans, the English, and my own countrymen.* We of the court came mostly into contact with the first; we had few dealings with the second, with the last none. The first could not do without their wine, to which they had been accustomed all their lives, and therefore utterly

* Welshmen, who formed the bulk of the first invaders.

declined to make any stay in the distant marches or
the castles which lay far from the sea. They cared
only to hang about the prince, and stuck closely to
his side, satisfied so long as they kept near the
supplies and ran no risk of scarcity. Grand talkers
and boasters these men, and full of strange oaths,
contemning with overweening pride all who were not
of them; yet withal not too proud to scramble for
wealth and land.* In short, they got all the honour,
but when there was any work to be done they were
not to be found.

Since then the original invaders, through whose
enterprise a way had been opened for us into the
island, were treated with suspicion and neglect, since
the counsels of the prince's advisers were communicated
exclusively to the new-comers, confidence was reposed
in them alone, they only deemed worthy of consideration, it came about that as the veterans held aloof and
lent no aid to those who did not appreciate its value,
these interlopers met with little success in anything
they undertook.

July 25th, A.D. 1186.—[Assassination of Hugh de Laci: English account].

Wilelm. Newburg. Hist. Rer. Anglic. 1186.

Hugh de Laci had disregarded the king's order [*in*
1184] to return, and stayed in Ireland. . . . But after
a while, as though the jealousy of fortune had been
aroused on behalf of the king of the English, Hugh

---

* So, too, in Campion they are "great quaffers, lourdens,
proud belly-swaines, fed with extortion and bribery."

became the victim of treachery, and met his end at the hands of a certain youth, one of the friendly Irish in his employ. For it fell upon a day that he went out of his castle for a country walk, and became separated about a stone's throw from his attendants; when as he chanced to stoop to point out something or other on the ground, the traitor, overjoyed at finding the opportunity he had long sought, swung his axe down like lightning with all his might upon his master's neck. Off flew the head of the great captain. The attendants rushed up to avenge the deed, but in vain, for the assassin, who was an active young fellow, got away under cover of a neighbouring wood and escaped.

It is said that the king of the English, who at the time was in a remote part of his dominions, exhibited the greatest satisfaction at the news of this event; and the affairs of Ireland were subsequently administered by him with greater caution.*

July 25th, A.D. 1186.—[Assassination of Hugh de Laci: Irish account].

Annals of the Four Masters: 1186; *O'Donovan's Translation from the Irish.*

"Hugo de Laci, the profaner and destroyer of many churches; lord of the English of Meath, Breifny and Uriel; he to whom the tribute of Connaught was paid; he who had conquered the greater part of

---

* That is the king was careful in future not to grant to any of his vassals in Ireland such extraordinary powers as de Laci had enjoyed.

Ireland for the English, and of whose English castles all Meath, from the Shannon to the sea, was full; after having finished the castle of Durrow [*in N. of King's co.*] set out accompanied by three Englishmen to view it. One of the men of Teffia [*a district in co. Westmeath*], a youth named Gillagan-inathar O'Meyey, approached him and drawing out an axe, which he had kept concealed, with one blow of it severed his head from his body; and both head and trunk fell into the ditch of the castle. This was in revenge of Columbkille. Gillagan-inathar fled, and, by his fleetness of foot, made his escape from the English and Irish to the wood of Kilclare [*in King's co.*]."

A.D. 1186.—[A defeat of John de Courci].

Annals of Boyle: 1186.

A victory was gained over John de Courci at Tegas,* where, with others, 16 English barons were slain, and [the foreigners] returned home in great confusion. Murchard Mac Fergail and . . . many more fell [on the Irish side].

[Some results of the conquest.]

Gervas. Tilb.

Ireland . . . was inhabited in unbroken course by Scottish septs [*clans*] down to the times of the illustrious Henry [II], king of the English, your grand-

* Mr. Hennessy writes that this is a mistake for " Segais," the old name of the Curlieu Mountains, between Roscommon and Sligo counties, and near Boyle.

sire, most worshipful prince.* He was the first monarch to drive from their lands the loathsome Irish tribes, and to allot the conquered territory to Englishmen on feudal tenure, though it had not been gained without considerable loss of life to the English and Welsh invaders. Whence it has come to pass that a country whose inhabitants from the remotest ages drew their chief sustenance from milk, neglected the duty of fasting during Lent, devoured flesh raw, led unclean lives, and contemned the obligations of religion, is now strong in an awakened sense of piety among its people. And although it has been the last corner of Christendom to take to true godliness, and that too under compulsion, yet to-day, in comparison with other nations, for strict adherence to holy observances and intensity of devout fervour it holds the first place. It rejoices in a hierarchy with settled sees, abounds in monasteries which are well conducted, teems with flourishing estates and good entertainment.

(The Strongbow episode can now be considered fairly over, though its effects had lingered on for a season after the death of the earl. From about this time a new phase of affairs may be said to begin: a phase marked by anarchy even more hopeless than before. The "conquest" had been too fitful and too feebly supported to be in any sense complete. The invaders definitely split into two parties, a state of things which we have seen foreshadowed in the disobedience of de Laci in 1184 and in the 36th chapter of the IInd Book of Gerald's *Expugnatio*. The needy condition of the adventurers and of many of the royal

---

* The emperor Otto iv, to whom the work of Gervase of Tilbury is dedicated.

officers, the distance from England, and the fact that the English kings were never able to find leisure to apply themselves properly to Irish matters, encouraged most of the English in Ireland to set up as independent chieftains, and allowed them to do so with impunity. The population of the island, amidst a turmoil of strife and confusion, finally settled down into three divisions: but there was no peace in the land. There were (1) the loyal inhabitants of the Pale, which became a string of counties palatine along the eastern coast. They lived under English law, but were relatively few in number; (2) the Anglo-Irish rebels in the open country: the "*ipsis Hibernis Hiberniores*;" (3) the "mere Irish," the Kelt-Iberian natives, in the west and the mountains, who maintained a perpetual guerilla warfare with everybody, including themselves. Except the "five bloods" they lived according to the old Brehon law.

So it went on through a long period of neglect, broken only by the futile attempts of Richard II. and some rough handling by Henry VIII., till the latter part of Elizabeth's reign. found a sovereign free to attend to Ireland.

It is to be remarked that in England the Teuton has absorbed the Kelt, while in Ireland the Kelt-Iberian has always to all intents and purposes absorbed the Teuton. The Danish and Norman invasions of England were vigorous movements which benefited the country in the end, whereas the Norwegian and Anglo-Norman invasions of Ireland were comparatively weak and ill-sustained efforts which seem only to have served to aggravate the disorder in the island.)

How the Irish race might be completely conquered.

Girald. Cambr. Expug. Hibern. Lib. II. cap. xxxviii.

Just as it is a general principle to trust a workman in his own craft, so it is a matter of common sense that in every warlike enterprise one should rely especially on the judgment of those who have come into familiar contact with the hostile country in similar undertakings, and are well acquainted with the character and customs of its inhabitants. Such men, too, are interested in giving their assistance to weaken or crush a people who in the course of a long war attended with many conflicts have come to regard them with deep and implacable hatred and hostility. And now I am on this subject, I may remark that it would have been a fortunate thing for the Welsh marches and the English settlers there, if the king had in his administration of those parts adopted such a policy, and checked the incursions of the neighbouring enemy. The new-comers are doubtless well-trained and excellent soldiers in their own land; but a campaign in France is a very different thing from a campaign in Ireland or Wales. In the former case it is carried on in an open country, in the latter in broken country; there we have plains, here woods; there armour is held in esteem, here it is reckoned cumbersome and out of place; there victory is won by weight, here by activity. In France the vanquished become prisoners and may be ransomed, in Ireland quarter is unknown and instant decapitation their fate. Wherefore, although when armies in serried array engage on level ground, the ordinary heavy and complicated panoply, whether it be wambais * or ring †

* Wadded or quilted linen armour. By the Assize of Arms in 1181 Henry II ordered every burgess to provide himself with lance, iron cap, and wambais, or gambeson as it is sometimes called.

† Under Henry II and Richard I the hauberk was made of iron ring-mail, as also were the "chausses," or leg and foot armour.

armour, is a noble adornment as well as a protection to the soldier, yet when the fighting is to be confined to passes, woods and bogs, where footmen are more serviceable than cavalry, a light equipment is far better. For against an unarmoured enemy whose chance of victory rests solely on the success of his first onslaught,* lightly armed soldiers are quite sufficient; as in such a case agile men fleeing among defiles or over difficult ground can only be pursued and routed by troops, with superior arms and outfit it is true, but at the same time accoutred in such a way as to admit of perfect ease and freedom of movement. It is no wonder, therefore, that our heavy men-at-arms, with their complex suits of mail and their deeply curved saddles, experience great difficulty in dismounting, still more in re-mounting, and find it almost impossible to act with any effect as footsoldiers, whenever the occasion requires it.

The fittest men, then, for any expedition in Ireland or Wales are those born and bred in the Welsh marches; men practised in the frontier warfare of that region. Brought up in this kind of life, they are both venturesome and fleet of foot. As the exigencies of war demand, they are in turn apt horsemen or active infantry. In matters of food and drink rough fare is no hardship to them, and at a push they will cheerfully endure privation. These were the men who made the first essay in Ireland, and these also must be the men to finally complete its conquest.

* Compare the tactics of the Highlanders, even so late as "The '45," and that of the Zulus at the Cape.

One must, however,—
> Fitly to each its separate part assign :
> Each to its part with jealous care confine.*

For I admit that against heavy and fully armoured troops, arrayed for fight in a champaign country and whose prospects of victory lie entirely in their personal strength and the ponderous weight of their harness and war-gear, you must oppose soldiers of a similar character. In like manner a nimble light infantry acting in rugged country must be met by infantry as mobile as itself and used to that style of warfare.

In the Irish wars, moreover, this, too, must certainly not be overlooked : that archers be always stationed between each troop of cavalry, in order that their shafts may keep at a distance the slingers who, alternately advancing and retreating with great speed, pelt with stones our unwieldy men-at-arms.

Besides, this side of the country as far as the Shannon, which river separates the three eastern divisions of the island from the fourth or western part, should be thickly sown with castles and so strengthened and protected. The more distant regions, Connaught that is and Munster beyond Shannon, ought to be kept under for the present by the exaction of an annual tribute. Limerick, however, must be excepted, as it is indispensable that this city be again taken and held. It were better, far better, at first to set up our strongholds by degrees in suitable places, and to carry out a coherent system of castle-building, feeling the

* Hor. *A. P.* 92.

way, so to speak, at every step, than to erect large numbers at wide intervals and without any set plan, for such have no unity or centre and can be of no support to each other at critical times.

How Ireland should be governed.
Girald. Cambr. Expug. Hibern. Lib. II. cap. xxxix.

Inasmuch as the loyalty of the Irish is precarious and they are prone to insubordination, no less light of mind than light of foot, just as care is needed in conquering them, so when conquered they must be ruled with a wise discretion. The management of the country ought to be given to men who are firm, strict, and unwavering of purpose. In times of tranquillity, when the natives abide contentedly by the laws as dutiful subjects, their governors should win their confidence by keeping good faith and treating them with marked respect. But whenever, at the promptings of their natural fickleness, they dare to break the peace, immediately all appearance of mildness must be put aside and sharp chastisement follow at once upon the offence. When they have settled down again into order, and condign satisfaction has been taken for their misdeeds, since—

> 'Tis meet that time slay wrath : th' ungenerous soul
> Keeps green the memory of a buried strife,

so long as they continue in obedience, let their former transgressions be forgotten, let them enjoy the same amount of freedom and the same consideration as at first. By this method their interest would lie in mantaining an orderly habit of life and seeking the advantages of quiet, while the certainty of a speedy and inevitable punishment would act as a deterrent from rash attempts.

But rulers who mingle right and wrong; who give way to law-breakers, but oppress the loyal; are all complaisance to those who threaten war, but prey on those who keep the peace; despoil the unwarlike but truckle to the rebellious, as we have seen many governors of Ireland do: such men by confounding all things committed to their charge are at length themselves confounded.

Besides, since ills foreguarded against lose half their power of hurt, let the prudent procurator seize the opportunity in times of calm to strengthen his position and prepare against the dangers of an always possible war by raising castles and clearing the forest roads; for this vindictive race is ever plotting treason under the mask of friendship. Wherefore, too, since it is well to take warning from the mishaps of others and to learn therefrom what it is profitable to eschew— for where there is foreknowledge the blow may miss its aim—the instances of those illustrious men Milo de Cogan, Ralph of youthful promise, Hugh de Laci, and Roger Poer, show that one is never safe from the Irish axe.* For, as my *Topography* shows, in dealing with this deceitful nation, their perfidy is far more to be feared than their prowess, their peaceful professions than their vapouring valour, their plausible vows than

* Which, docked of its head, is the modern shillelagh.

their poisonous venom, their spite than their soldiership, their treason than their tactics, their falsity as friends than their fighting power as foes.

Also, as Evodius says, 'The calamities of former generations are a lesson to posterity, and past error is a warning for all time.' Since, then, in the case of this people over-watchfulness can do no harm, nay, the most careful precautions scarce suffice, as soon as they have been completely subjected, a public edict should, as among the Sicilians,* forbid on pain of the severest penalty all bearing of arms. Meanwhile during peace they ought not to be allowed to carry at any time or place that detestable instrument of treachery † which by an old but evil custom is always in their hands as a staff might be.

To conclude, whereas Ireland is on many just grounds, the main points of which I have set forth above,‡ portion of the dominions of the kings of Britain; and forasmuch as without the advantages of commercial intercourse with the latter island, the former cannot subsist, it seems fitting that upon the conquered land there should be imposed a tribute payable in gold § or the birds ‖ in which it abounds,

* After the conquest of Sicily by the Normans. Similar complaints were made of the treachery of the Sicilians towards their conquerors.
  † The hand-axe.   ‡ Bk. II. chap. 33.
§ The demand for gold is at first sight surprising, but there is evidence that the precious metals, especially gold, were then comparatively plentiful in Ireland. The records show that dues, rents, ransoms and donations to the church were often paid in sums of gold [reckoned by weight] considerable for those times.

K

146   DESCRIPTION OF THE IRISH.

whereby all likelihood of ill-will and discord may be removed. And as the ages roll on and the line of our royal house is perpetuated generation after generation, let the memory of this conquest be kept fresh by that tribute being made an annual one, as a lasting testimony to the glory and greatness of the king and kingdom of Great Britain.

Of the character, customs, and external appearance of the Irish.

Girald. Cambr. Top. Hibern. Dis. III. cap. x.

I have thought it not superfluous to lay before my reader a brief description of this people as regards both their persons and their minds : that is to say the external and the internal peculiarities they present.

In this country children are not, as elsewhere, delicately brought up ;* for everything over and above the homely and somewhat scanty nourishment they receive from their rude parents is left to nature. They are laid in no cradle, nor swathed in swaddling clothes; their tender limbs know not the use of the warm bath, neither are they adjusted with the help of art. Yet Nature, as if to show what her unaided power can do, fails not to rear and mould them through

Where it originally came from is not clear; whether from the old Irish mines, or from the ancient intercourse with Spain and the East, or from commerce with the Ostman pirates and settlers : perhaps from all these sources and others of which we know nothing.

‖ Probably falcons for hawking are especially meant here.

DESCRIPTION OF THE IRISH. 147

infancy and childhood, until in the fulness of time she leads each to man's estate conspicuous for a tall and handsome form, regular features, and a fresh complexion.

But although adorned to the full with such natural gifts as these, still the barbarous fashion of their garments, their shaggy beards, and their ignorance reveal the arrant savage. For little do they wear in the way of woollen clothing, and that little black (which is the colour of the sheep of the country) and of ungainly cut: their habit being to apparel themselves in small closely-fitting hoods extending over the shoulders and down to the elbow, generally made of parti-coloured scraps sewn together. Under this instead of a coat they have a gown. Woollen trews complete their attire, being breeches and hose in one, usually dyed some tint.

In riding they use no saddles, high boots, or spurs; but simply carry a rod crooked at the end, with which they both urge on and guide their horses. Reins indeed they have, yet they perform the double duty of bit and bridle: thus the horses, which feed on nothing but grass, can browse at any time.

They go to battle without armour, which they regard as an encumbrance: and in fact think it a sign of valour and an honour to fight without such protection. Of weapons they use but three kinds: short spears and pairs of darts—and in this they follow the custom of the Basques—, while they have learnt also from the Norwegians and Ostmen (of whom later) the use of the great battle-axe, and excellently well

DESCRIPTION OF THE IRISH.

wrought and tempered their axes are. They wield them with one hand only instead of both, laying the thumb along the upper side of the haft and so directing the blow. From the stroke of one of these neither the cone-shaped helmet is sufficient to guard the head, nor a shirt of ring-mail the body. Thus in our own time it happened that a soldier had his thigh cut right through with one stroke of an axe, encased though it was all round in good steel,* the amputated leg falling to the ground on one side of the horse, and its dying owner on the other. When arms fail they cast stones, with which they can inflict much damage on an enemy, as they are handier and readier at slinging than any other nation.

Verily a wild and inhospitable race : living only on the produce of their beasts, and living like beasts themselves. A race but little advanced from the primitive pastoral life. For whereas the stages of human progress are from the forest to the field, from the field to the town, and so to civic polity, this people despising agricultural labour, having little taste for the refinements of civilization, and showing a strong aversion from political institutions, knows not how to relinquish the sylvan and bucolic habits to which it has always been accustomed.

They put their cattle out to graze anywhere, for there are no enclosures and the pasture itself is not uniformly luxuriant. Cultivated ground is rarely seen, sown land hardly ever. This scarcity of tilled soil is

* This was, however, the feat of a Norseman, as related on p. 42.

Danish Axe, *circa* 900-950. Found in Mammen, Jutland. The Irish learnt the use of the battle-axe from the Norse invaders.

due to the neglect of those who ought to till it; for much of the surface of the country is naturally fertile and productive.

Veins of various kinds of metal abound in the earth, but owing to the same criminal indolence they are not worked or turned to account. Gold, for which the natives thirst to an extent that betrays their Iberian origin, is brought hither by the chapmen who scour the seas in search of commerce.

Moreover they do not employ their time in the manufacture of linen, cloth, or any other ware, nor in the development of a single mechanic art. They are simply the slaves of ease and sloth : freedom from exertion they esteem the height of luxury, freedom from restraint the summit of wealth.

Wherefore this race is a race of savages: I say again a race of utter savages. For not merely are they uncouth of garb, but they also let their hair and beards grow to an outrageous length, something like the new-fangled fashion which has lately come in with us. In short, all their ways are brutish and unseemly.

But customs are formed by intercourse, and since in these remote parts men are so far withdrawn from the rest of the world, and come so little into contact with refined and civilized nations that they might be in a different planet, small wonder if they know nothing beyond the barbarism in which they have been born and nurtured, and which cleaves to them like a second nature.

The Creator has done His part in giving them of His best; but where there is any call for effort on their part they are worthless.

Of the matchless skill of this nation in instrumental music.

Girald. Cambr. Top. Hibern. Dis. III. cap. xi.

It is only in instrumental music that I find any commendable diligence in this nation : but in that art they incomparably excel every other people that I have met. For their execution is not, like that which we hear in Britain, slow and laboured, but adroit and sprightly, while their tone is full and the refrain of their melodies sweet and gay. . . . Harmonies which afford deep and inexpressible mental delight to a man whose ear has been educated to grasp their subtleties and to enter into the mysteries of musical science, weary rather than please one whose sense of melody is untrained, who, as it were, 'seeing doth not perceive and hearing doth not understand.' To the latter all profoundly modulated symphonies cause a feeling of irksomeness and even repugnance, for they seem to be no better than noise without order, method, or meaning.

It must be remarked, however, that both Scotland and Wales strive emulously to rival Ireland in music ; the former on account of affinity of race, the latter because of their mutual proximity and intercourse. Ireland, indeed, uses and takes pleasure in two instruments alone : the lute and the timbrel ; Scotland in three, the lute, the timbrel, and the crowd ; Wales in the lute, the treble and bass pipes, and the crowd. The Irish, by the way, make their strings not of leather but of brass. Many, however, think that

Scotland has not only equalled her teacher, Ireland, in musical skill, but has even far surpassed her, and now look to the former country as the fount of the harmonic art.

Music with its gladsome strains not only yields pleasure, but, more than this, is of real service to us. For in no small measure does it help to cheer the saddened heart, brighten the clouded face, smooth the frowning brow, banish the crabbed mien, and promote in every one hilarity again. Of all the most charming things in life, nothing gives more solace and enjoyment to the soul of man.

Two delights there are which refresh and enliven the human sense: sweet sounds and scents. Indeed our faculties may be said, as it were, to feed on fragrance and on harmony.

No matter to what subject the mind may be applied, music quickens the intellect, and though by insensible means still with sensible results stimulates the perception. It excites both the valour of the brave, and the pious aspirations of the devout. Hence it was that the bishops and abbots and holy men in Ireland were wont to carry their lutes with them on their journeyings, and found a godly joy in song and tune. Wherefore St. Kevin's harp is held by the natives in no small reverence as a holy and honourable relic to this very day. So, too, the bray of the war-horn awakes a response in the warrior's breast, and when its loud blast proclaims the signal for attack, an answering impulse rouses to even greater daring the spirit of the brave.

At times, indeed, music acts in contrary ways on different temperaments or varies in its effect according to the mood of the hearer; for it may inflame the passions of the vicious as well as fire the prowess of the valiant or the virtue of the good. It is said of Alexander of Macedon that once as he sat at meat with his friends, there fell upon his ear the soft notes of a lyre, when he forthwith rose and cut the strings. On being asked his reason for the act, he replied 'Better that harp-strings be severed than heart-strings.' For he felt—and in this he took account of the weakness of humanity—that his emotions, struggle as he might, would by such dulcet tones be irresistibly excited as the festive moment suggested: that under the influence of melody he would be drawn to weakness (to which perhaps he was already inclined) rather than to warfare, luxury than labour, venery than virtue, sensuality than self-control; since assuredly our feelings are by no means submissive to our will.

In addition to this, music soothes in sickness and in fatigue. Its sounds, outside us as they are, still operate within, so as to either quite cure the malady or at least help us to bear it with greater patience. It is, therefore, a comforter to all, a physician to many, since there are no sufferings which it does not alleviate and some it cures. It was the harp of David that restrained the unclean spirit from vexing Saul: and ever while he played the devil was at rest, and ever when he ceased the devil tare him afresh.

The words of Solomon, however, 'Music is out of

ON MUSIC. 153

place in time of mourning," * seem to be opposed to what I say. Doubtless he who unasked introduces song in the midst of grief, or affecting joy in the very moment of affliction bursts into exultant melody, must be either a Stoic or a fool. But though no strong feeling of distress admits of consolation while still fresh and perhaps increasing, yet Time is the great comforter, and under his healing touch little by little does sorrow lose its sting. The mourner whose sadness reason cannot mitigate nor medicine cure will find his dole unedged, his pain slackened with the lapse of years: years that bring an end to every ill. For human nature is so constituted that the things of this life are always on the increase or the decrease, always progressing or declining: to stand still is not within their power; and on reaching a summit straightway they fall with a velocity far greater than that with which they rose. This being so, if you watch the times and carefully guide your course by circumstances, your words and actions instead of being out of season will be suited to each occasion.

> Who but a fool will chide a mother's tears
> Shed o'er the bier of a well-loved son?
> Not such a time for pitiless rebuke.†

Therefore—

> Let the full tide of grief flow unopposed,
> Which till it ebb admits not of a cure.†

Thus we see that music has a twofold influence:

* Eccles. xxii. 6.
† Adapted from Ovid, *Rem. Am.* 127, 128; 119.

by its aid the mind may be roused or lulled. Agreeably to this the Irish and Spaniards and certain other nations introduce dirges amid their lamentations for the dead, which may either help them to more intensely realize the bitterness of their loss when recent, or perchance allay their anguish when the first shock is past.

'Song, too, cheers us in our daily tasks; oft does a ditty refresh the dull routine of toil.' * Times and again have we heard the craftsman lightening his labour with some homely lay.

'The very beasts, to say nothing of snakes, and birds, and seals, are allured by melody.' * And, what is even more marvellous, music will recall to their hive a migrating swarm of bees and make them settle there. I have sometimes myself, when on a voyage, seen seals follow in the wake of the ship for a long distance, and raise themselves bodily out of the water and prick up their ears to listen to the sound of a trumpet or a harp.

Moreover, as Isidorus says, 'without music no education can be complete: for music and harmony are all around us. Creation itself may be said to be in one aspect a kind of harmony: the heavens themselves revolve under laws of harmony.' *

*   *   *   *   *

I have greatly enjoyed this digression, nor do I think it was wholly uncalled for.

* Isid. *Orig.* iii. 16.

Of the villainy and foul duplicity of the Irish.

Girald. Cambr. Top. Hibern. Dis. III. cap. xx.

The Irish are beyond all other nations given to treachery: they hold to their bond with no one. While expecting absolute good faith from others, their own word, their oath, given though it may have been under the most solemn sanctions of religion, they daily violate without shame or fear. So even when you have taken the greatest forethought for your protection from danger or from loss by receiving pledges and hostages, when you have firmly, as you think, cemented the obligations of friendship, conferred every kindness in your power, and apparently made all safe with the utmost vigilance, then begin to fear; for then especially is their malice on the watch for its chance, since they foresee that, owing to the very multitude of your precautions, you will not be on the watch yourself.

Then will they fly to their foul arts, then to the weapons of guile the use of which they know so well, hoping in your fond confidence to find their opportunity of striking an unexpected blow.

Of the axe, which they ever bear in their hands, as though it might be a staff

Girald. Cambr. Top. Hibern. Dis. III. cap. xxi.

By an old, rather I should say an ill custom, at all times they have in their hands an axe instead of a staff; so as to be always prepared to carry their fell designs into effect. Wherever they go, this is their inseparable companion. When they espy and decide to seize the looked-for occasion, this weapon has not to be drawn like a sword, stretched like a bow, or brought to the charge like a lance : no preparation is needed, it has just to be raised a little and the fatal blow can be inflicted. Thus they have always at hand, nay, in hand, and ready, the means of dealing death. From this axe there is no security: foolhappy you go on in your assurance of safety and— down comes the stroke. Permit the carrying of the axe, and you run heedlessly into risk : your blood be on your own head.

Of a strange and monstrous way of inaugurating a king.

Girald. Cambr. Top. Hibern. Dis. III. cap. xxv.

There are some things which shame would oblige me to suppress, were it not that in pursuing my subject I am bound to relate them. For an unsavoury episode, though it may afford an opportunity for the play of wit, still seems in some sort to defile the narrator. Howbeit, the severity of history forbids me to shrink from truth or spare my modesty; yet I trust that pure lips may tell a degrading fact in passably decent words.

Well, there is in the extreme north of Ulster, that is in Tyrconnel, a certain tribe which is accustomed to inaugurate its kings with the following most barbarous and abominable ceremony. When all the inhabitants of the district have met together, a white mare is led forward into the midst of the assembly. The sovereign-designate then enters the circle on all fours, in full view of every one, and crawls up to the animal: thus conducting himself not like a prince but like a beast of the field, not as a king but a savage, and by this act of folly and disgrace confessing himself to be no better than a brute. Then the mare is slaughtered, cut up, and boiled on the spot, and a bath prepared out of the liquid for the monarch-elect. As he sits in it, the flesh of the mare is handed to him: of this he partakes, and the people stand round and join in the repast. The gravy, too, in which he is bathing he quaffs, not using a cup or even his hands, but lapping and sucking it up in large draughts beast-fashion with his mouth. When these rites, or rather wrongs, are completed his royal authority is thereby confirmed.*

Of the many unbaptized in the island, who have not yet arrived at the knowledge of the faith.

Girald. Cambr. Top. Hibern. Dis. III. cap. xxvi.

Although our religion was founded in this land so long ago, and has prospered in it too, yet in some

* It is well to add that Irish antiquaries indignantly deny the truth of all this. It may be one of many cases in which Gerald's credulity was imposed upon by his native informants; yet even then it is probable that a reference to some pre-Aryan pagan ceremony underlies the story. The fact of the *mare* being used may indicate a survival from matriarchal customs. These things are ornamented often enough and highly enough, but they are rarely inventions pure and simple. *Cf.* Elton, *Origin of English History*, for analogous British customs.

corners of the island there are still to be found numbers of persons who have never been baptized, and whom through the negligence of their pastors the knowledge of the faith has never reached. For some sailors have told me that one Lent-tide, being driven by stress of weather to the great unexplored seas off the north of Connaught, they at length took shelter under the lee of a small island; and even there their anchors hardly held though they had three cables out. By the third day, however, the wind had fallen, the sky was fair again and the sea calm, and they then descried at no great distance a coast, the outlines of which were entirely strange to them. Presently they made out a little coracle paddling towards them from

Modern Irish Coracle. From Mr. S. C. Hall's *Ireland*.

the shore. It was narrow and rather long, constructed of wicker-work and covered outside with hides, which were sewn to the frame. In it were two men, stark naked, except that they had on girdles of undressed pelts. They resembled the Irish in having long tawny hair, but theirs fell below their shoulders and overspread a great part of their bodies. The sailors on finding that they spoke Irish and hearing that they were of some part of Connaught invited them on board, when they appeared struck with wonder at all they beheld, as though everything were quite new to them. For they stated that never before had they seen a big ship, or one built of wood, or such articles of workmanship as met their eyes there; and when bread and cheese was offered them, they refused to taste such strange food, for so it was to them. They told how they lived on nothing but flesh, and fish, and milk; and how they wore no clothes, save sometimes the skins of beasts when the cold was most intense. Then they asked the shipmen whether they had meat for them, and on being admonished that it was not lawful to eat meat in Lent, it was clear that they were utterly ignorant what Lent might be. Whereupon they were asked whether they were Christians and had been baptized, but they said that they knew nothing of Christ, nor till that hour had ever heard His name. And when they went away, they took with them a loaf and a piece of cheese, that they might astonish their neighbours by showing them the victuals that the strangers ate.

Of the clergy of Ireland and how they are praiseworthy in many respects.

Girald. Cambr. Top. Hibern. Dis. III. cap. xxvii.

Let us now turn to the clerical order. The clergy of this land are well enough in point of piety, and possess many virtues, among which conspicuous above all is continence. They are scrupulously regular also in the performance of the psalms, hours, lessons, and prayers, for they keep within the precincts of their foundations and devote themselves entirely to their sacred duties. In the matter of abstemiousness in diet they are not sparing of themselves, for most of them as a rule fast every day till after compline, even until dusk. Ah, but would to God that after their long abstinence they were themselves as sober as their supper is late, as genuinely temperate as they are grave of talk, as free from guzzling as they are from guttling, no more topers in fact than in face. Among so many thousands you will scarcely find a single one who after this perseverance in fasting and orison does not make up for the hardships of the day by indulging at night to a most unseemly extent in wine and various other liquors. So, as if they divided the twenty-four hours into two equal parts, allotting the day-time to the spirit, the night-time to the flesh, they give themselves during the hours of light to the works of light, during the hours of darkness to the works of darkness.

Of a sarcastic retort of the archbishop of Cashel.

Girald. Cambr. Top. Dis. III. cap. xxxii.

I once, in the presence of Gerard a clerk of the Roman Church, then sent as legate to Ireland, raised these and similar objections * to Maurice, archbishop of Cashel, a discreet and learned man, and threw the blame of the low standard of morality in that land especially upon the prelates. I drew, too, a very strong argument from the fact that no one in that kingdom had ever through his zeal for the Church of God won the crown of martyrdom. The archbishop answered by a side-thrust, witty enough, though not to the point. 'Very true,' he said, 'because although our people may seem rude, fierce, and barbarous, yet they have always paid great honour and reverence to ecclesiastics, and have never on any occasion raised their hands against God's holy saints. But now there have come into the island men of a nation that knows how to make martyrs and is accustomed to do it. Henceforth Ireland, like other countries, will have its martyrs.' †

* Concerning the attitude of the Irish bishops, whom Gerald accuses of leading a monastic life and neglecting their pastoral duties. Most of them, in fact, were elected from out of the monasteries, not from among the secular clergy.

† The archbishop was alluding to the recent murder of Becket.

Of a great lake which had a miraculous origin.

Girald. Cambr. Top. Dis. II. cap. ix.

In Ulster there is a lake of marvellous size, being 30 miles long and 15 broad,* and out of it flows a most beautiful river, called the Bann, which empties itself into the Northern ocean. . . . It is said that this lake came into existence owing to a dire and wondrous calamity.

There lived in a region now covered by the mere a race of men who had long been sunk in vice. At that time it was a common saying among the country-folk that as soon as a certain fount in those parts should be left uncovered (for, from the respect shown it on account of a savage superstition, it was kept closed and sealed), the spring would immediately well over and vomit forth a mighty stream that would inundate the whole neighbourhood and sweep away its inhabitants. Now it happened that one day a young woman went to this fountain to draw water, when just as she had filled her pitcher, her child, whom she had left a little way off, began to cry, and with a mother's anxiety she ran at once to him without staying to first seal up the spring again. "The voice of the people is the voice of God," for immediately after as the woman was hurrying back to finish fastening up the spring, she was met by such a rush of water which had burst out of it, that not only she and her boy forthwith, but within the space of an hour all the denizens of the valley with their cattle

* Lough Neagh.

Round Tower at the Rock of Cashel.

and everything were swallowed up in this, as it were, partial or local deluge. And when the wealth of waters had fully hidden the whole face of that region, they ceased to pour forth and the flood remained there as a mighty lake; as if the Author of Nature judged the district which had seen such wickedness to be unfit for the habitation not only of its original owners, but for mankind in general for all time.*

That the tradition of this occurrence is true seems to be fairly confirmed by the fact that in calm weather the fishermen see plainly standing in the depths of the lake round ecclesiastical towers, tall and slender, like those they have in Ireland : † and oftentimes will they point these out to the wondering stranger as they ferry him across the lough.

* The date assigned to this in the Irish Annals is A.D. 62 ; the year after the death of Boadicea in Britain. A similar account is given of the origin of lough Foyle and of lough Erne. These traditions probably point to some volcanic phenomena. As late, indeed, as A.D. 1490 we find in the Four Masters an entry to the effect that lough Easkey, in Sligo, was suddenly formed in like manner by an "eruption of the earth."

† These are the famous round towers of Ireland concerning the origin and purpose of which there has been so much controversy. The reader will call to mind Moore's song :—

"On Lough Neagh's banks as the fisherman strays,
"When the clear, cold eve's declining,
"He sees the Round Towers of other days,
"In the wave beneath him shining."

Irish Melodies.

Of the Giants' Dance, which was taken over from Ireland to Britain.

Girald. Cambr. Top. Hibern. Dis. II. cap. xviii.

In ancient times there was in Ireland a remarkable pile of stones, known as the Giants' Dance,* because the giants had brought them into Ireland from the farthest limits of Africa, and partly by mechanical contrivances, partly by sheer strength, had set them up in a marvellous manner on the plain of Kildare, not far from Naas. Hence there may be seen in the same spot to this day some of these stones exactly like the rest [on Salisbury Plain] and erected in a similar fashion.

It is wonderful how so many stones of such vast size were got together into one place or raised into an edifice when there. Whatever machinery could have been used to hoist upon stones so huge and high lintels formed of others no less in bulk? The latter, too, are poised in such a way that they seem to hang in mid-air, and to be rather balanced in their places by the skilful disposition of the architect than supported by the tops of the uprights.

According to the British History,† Aurelius Ambrosius, king of the Britons, had these stones removed from Ireland into Britain through the divine agency of Merlin [Ambrosius]; and in order that some notable memorial of so mighty an exploit might remain, they

* Stonehenge.
† *i.e.* the *Historia Britonum* of Geoffrey of Monmouth: viii. 10-12.

were arranged in the same relative position as they had occupied when in Ireland on the spot where the flower of Britain fell under the treacherous knives of the Saxons, where the too confiding British warriors met their end by the weapons of perfidy wielded under cover of a pretended peace.*

Of reptiles and the lack of them in Ireland, and how no venomous creatures are found there.

Girald. Cambr. Top. Hibern. Dis. I. cap. xxviii.

Among all the various species of reptiles Ireland is happy in possessing only those that are harmless, for venomous creatures do not exist in the island. There are no vipers or snakes of any kind, no toads, frogs, tortoises, scorpions, or dragons. Spiders, however, are found, as are leeches and lizards, but these are entirely innocuous. Whence it may be said, or even seriously stated in writing, pleasantly enough, and with truth as well, that in Gaul and Italy the frogs deafen one with their croaking, that in Britain they are mute, while in Ireland there are none.

Some persons, indeed, conjecture, by what is

---

* An incident in the legend of the Jutish conquest of Kent. Hengist had invited Vortigern and the British nobles to a conference and feast at which all the Britons except Vortigern were assassinated. If anything of the kind ever happened, the sacred site of Stonehenge might well have been chosen as the place of meeting. It is noticeable that Gerald regards the tradition of the massacre as the memorial of Merlin's exploit, not the edifice as the monument of the massacre.

probably a flattering figment, that St. Patrick * and other native saints cleared the island of all living things that were poisonous. But history asserts with greater probability that from primæval times, and long before the first foundations of the faith were laid in Ireland, that country, owing to something being wanting in the soil or vegetation, has always been devoid of reptiles as it is of certain other productions of nature.

Now to my mind there is nothing to be wondered at in the fact that this land is naturally deficient in reptiles, for so also it is in some kinds of fish, and birds, and beasts. But it is really astonishing that no venomous creature imported from elsewhere has ever been able to live here, and this is so still. For we read in the ancient writings of the saints of the country that on divers occasions for the sake of the experiment snakes were brought over in brazen pots; but as soon as the ships had crossed the middle of the Irish Sea, the animals were found to be dead. Poison, too, in like manner, on being shipped over lost its venom in mid voyage under the influence of a kindlier atmosphere.

Bede, moreover, in writing of Ireland touches on

---

* Although St. Patrick is here called a native saint, it must be remembered that it is unknown from what country he originally came, though probably it was Gaul. He was first brought to Ireland as a slave. His death took place at an advanced age in 493, and his saint's day is March 17th. He thus flourished at the time of the early Teutonic settlements in Britain.

this subject as follows * :—'In Ireland you will see no reptile, no snake can exist there. For often have such been conveyed thither from Britain, nevertheless no sooner does the vessel near the Irish coast than they perish, killed by the scent of the air blown from the shore. Nay, almost everything produced in the island contains an antidote to poison.'

I have heard sea-going merchants state that now and again when unloading in Irish ports they have come across toads in the holds of their ships, and on throwing them alive on to the land, they at once turned on their backs, and in the presence of a crowd of wondering bystanders burst their bellies and died.

Wherefrom it seems proven that either through the beneficence of the saints, as is the general belief throughout the world, or from the strange and unparalleled but truly favourable action of the climate, or owing to some occult peculiarity in the soil itself inimical to poisons, no venomous creatures can subsist here, and anything noxious from other parts at once loses its virulent properties.

How the dust of this land is fatal to poisonous reptiles.

Girald. Cambr. Top. Hibern. Dis. I. cap. xxx.

To such an extent indeed is this land antagonistic to venom, that if gardens or any places in other countries are sprinkled with its dust, poisonous reptiles are thereby expelled and will not re-enter them.†

* *Hist. Eccl.* I. 1.
† This belief survives among the Irish in Australia.

Of the shoe-latchets of Ireland, which are opposed to poisons.

Girald. Cambr. Top. Hibern. Dis. I. cap. xxxi.

The shoe-ties as well of this island, provided they be not of foreign manufacture but made at home out of the hides of beasts bred there, if scraped into water and so drunk, supply a sure remedy against the bites of snakes and toads.

I have seen with my own eyes a shoe-string of this kind straightened out and then placed round a toad in a complete circle as a practical test. When the animal reached the string and tried to get over it he immediately fell back as if stunned. Then he tried the opposite side, with the same result. Finally, on finding that he was surrounded by the thong, he fled from it as though it were pestilential, quickly scratched a hole with his feet in the centre of the circle and buried himself in the mud. Many persons witnessed this besides myself.

Nay more, according to the assertion of Bede, almost everything which comes from this island is efficacious against poisons. For he avers that he saw 'that in the case of some people who had been stung by snakes, the progress of the virus was at once arrested and all swelling reduced by drinking water with which had been mixed scrapings of the 'leaves of books brought from Ireland.'*

Again, it happened within our own days in the north of England that an adder crawled into the

* *Hist. Eccl.* I. I.

throat of a youth who was sleeping with his mouth open, and descended into his stomach, when the ungrateful reptile made an ill return to the host who had thus furnished him with a lodging, by continually gnawing and tearing at his vitals. This so affected the young man that in the agonies he suffered immediate dissolution seemed preferable to a life which was but a protracted death. After meals the snake would allow him a short respite from torture, but before them none. In vain did he try at all the holy shrines throughout England to obtain relief; at length adopting a wiser counsel he crossed to Ireland, where directly he had swallowed the health-giving waters and the food of that country, his deadly enemy expired, and the youth returned whole again with great joy to his native land.

Of a frog lately found in Ireland [circa A.D. 1179].

Girald. Cambr. Top. Hibern. Dis. I. cap. xxxii.

Nevertheless in our times a frog was discovered in a grassy mead near Waterford, and was taken alive into the justice-hall before the then governor, Robert Poer, in the presence of many other persons, both English and Irish. The English were considerably surprised, but the Irish inspected it with absolute astonishment. Then Donnell, king of Ossory, a man of sense for an Irishman, and faithful to us,* who chanced to be present, smote himself upon the head

* In 1176 we find him marching in alliance with Reimund to the relief of Limerick.

in anguish of soul, and uttered these words: 'That reptile is the bearer of ill news to Ireland.' He went on to say that it was certainly a token of the coming of the English, and of the impending conquest and annexation of his fatherland.

Now let no one presume to suppose that this creature was ever born in Ireland, because not here, as in other lands, 'does the mud contain the spawn which generates green frogs.'* Had it been so, they would have been found more often and in greater numbers, both before and after this. But perchance some tiny germ had been attracted by the heat of the atmosphere from the mire into the clouds, and so blown hither by the wind; or even the embryo reptile itself might have been drawn up into the bosom of some low-sailing cloudlet, and thus borne along till it was deposited on this alien and uncongenial soil. What is more likely, however, is that the animal had been brought over in a chance ship which had put in at a neighbouring harbour, and on being flung ashore had managed, since it was not venomous, to keep itself alive for a time.

Of the isle of Man, which inasmuch as it harbours poisonous reptiles is regarded as belonging to Britain.

Girald. Cambr. Top. Hibern. Dis. II. cap. xv.

There is an island, one of the more important among the lesser isles [of Great Britain], which is now

* Ov. *Met.* xv. 375.

called Man, but in times gone by Ewania, lying exactly in mid-sea between North Ireland and Britain.

Now it was a matter of much debate among the ancients to which of the above two countries this island rightly belonged. At length the question was settled in this wise. By way of trial some reptiles were taken over there, and when it was found that they survived the test, all agreed that it must be part of Britain.

> Of two islands, in one of which no one dies; while into the other no living creature of the female sex can enter.
>
> *Girald. Cambr. Top. Hibern.* Dis. II. cap. iv.

There is in North Munster a lake * which has two islands, one larger than the other. On the former stands a church, held of great sanctity from times remote : on the latter a chapel, devoutly served by a few celibates called Heaven-worshippers or God-worshippers [*Culdees*].

Into the greater isle no woman or female living thing ever enters but it forthwith dies. This has been proved again and again in the case of dogs and cats and other animals of that sex, which have frequently been taken thither as an experiment, and have fallen dead upon the spot. It is remarkable that of the birds of the country the cocks settle in vast numbers upon the bushes of this island, but the hens leave their mates there and fly by, seeming to know the

* Lough Cre, now a bog near Roscrea in Tipperary.

peculiar properties of the place and avoiding it as pestilential.

In the lesser isle no decease has ever occurred and no one can die a natural death. Wherefore it is known as the Land of the Living. Yet at times persons there are sore troubled by deadly sickness, and are miserably afflicted even to the point of dissolution. And when all hope of recovery is past, when the sufferers see that there is no prospect of the slightest improvement, when by the increase of their maladies they are tortured to such a degree that to die outright is preferable to dragging on a life of death, they have themselves ferried over to the greater island, where as soon as they touch land they breathe their last.

Of an island one part of which is frequented by good the other by evil spirits.

Girald. Cambr. Top. Hibern. Dis. II. cap. v.

In Ulster there is a lake* containing an island which is divided into two parts. One side of it, whereon stands a church of approved holiness, presents to the view a landscape of rare beauty; and its charm is heightened and rendered glorious beyond compare by the visits of angels and the presence of the local saints, both plainly manifest to the human eye.

The other side, which is exceeding rugged and hideous, is reputed to have been assigned as the

* Lough Derg, in Donegal, is meant.

PURGATORY OF ST. PATRICK. 173

resort of demons only, and to be the haunt where throngs of evil spirits visibly perform their orgies. This portion of the island has in it nine pits; and if haply any person may dare to pass the night in one of these (which it is well known that now and again some reckless men have ventured on), he is at once seized by the malignant fiends, and throughout that night tormented in such grievous sort, and racked with so many violent and indescribable tortures by fire, by water, and what not, that when morning comes hardly a spark of life is found left in his wretched body.

It is said that whosoever has borne these agonies in discharge of a penance, will not be called upon to undergo further punishments in hell, except he go on to commit greater iniquities than before.

This place is called by the inhabitants The Purgatory of St. Patrick. For that holy man had to convince an unbelieving race of the penalties which awaited the condemned in the infernal regions, and of the veritable and everlasting life reserved for the elect. Wherefore, the better to impress on the minds of these rude heathen by a mysterious faith a doctrine so strange to them and so opposed to their prejudices, his earnest prayers were rewarded by obtaining a striking and miraculous illustration upon this earth of both states, which was an invaluable lesson to a stiff-necked people.

Of an island where corpses exposed to the air do not decay.

Girald. Cambr. Top. Hibern. Dis. II. cap. vi.

There lies in the sea off the western coast of Connaught a certain island named Aran,* and sanctified, so they say, by St. Brendan. There human bodies are not buried, neither do they become corrupt; but are laid out in the open air, and remain fresh. There a man may recognize and gaze with wondering eyes upon his grandsire, great-grandsire, great-great-grandsire, and a long series of his ancestors extending far back into the past.

Of the wondrous nature of [some] fountains.

Girald. Cambr. Top. Hibern. Dis. II. cap. vii.

In Munster is a fountain wherein if any one bathe his hair immediately turns white. I have seen a man with one side of his beard which had been washed in its water perfectly white, while the other had preserved its natural dark colour. There is, on the other hand, a fountain in the further part of Ulster in which whoever dips will never become gray. I may add that this spring is frequented by women in large numbers, and by men too, who are wishful to avoid a hoary head.

* A mistake: the legend belongs not to Aran but to Inisgluair off Mullet in co. Mayo.

Of a fish which had three golden teeth.

Girald. Cambr. Top. Hibern. Dis. II. cap. x.

Not long before the coming of the English into the island there was caught at Carlingford, in Ulster, a fish of immense size and of a peculiar kind. Amongst other remarkable points about it, it had (so the story goes) three golden teeth, weighing together fifty ounces. I should be inclined to suppose, however, that these teeth by their yellowish tinge bore some external resemblance to gold rather than really were of that metal, and that the colour they assumed was perhaps a presage of the golden times of the conquest so soon to come. Moreover, in our days, a stag was taken in the forest of Durham in Greater Britain with every tooth in its head of a golden hue.

Of an island which at first floated, but was at length firmly fixed by means of fire.

Girald. Cambr. Top. Hibern. Dis. II. cap. xii.

Among other islands is one that has lately appeared and goes by the name of The Phantom Isle. It originated as follows :—One calm day, in full view of the astonished islanders, a considerable mass of earth rose to the surface of the sea where no land had ever been seen before. Some of them declared it was a whale, or similar huge marine monster. Others, who observed that it remained motionless, said : 'Nay, but it is dry ground.' In order, however, to clear up their doubts, certain picked young men of one of the islands adjacent to the object determined to row out to it in a boat. But when they got so near that they were just expecting to touch the bottom, the island vanished from their sight as though it had sunk into the sea. Yet next day there it was again, and again played the youths the same trick. Finally, on the third day, by the advice of one of the older men, on drawing nigh they let fly at it an arrow with some ignited substance attached, in consequence of which on landing they found it stationary and habitable.

This is one of many proofs that fire is always the greatest enemy to any kind of apparition. So it happens that they who have just seen spectres cannot look at its brightness without swooning. For fire, both by its position [in the sky] and by its nature is the noblest of the elements, a witness, as it were, of the hidden mysteries of heaven. The firmament is fiery, the planets are fiery; with fire did the bush burn, and was not burnt; in form of fiery tongues the Holy Ghost sat upon the apostles.

Of miracles; and first of the apples ... of St. Kevin.

Girald. Cambr. Top. Hibern. Dis. II. cap. xxviii.

Pass we now to miracles; and let us begin with St. Kevin, the illustrious confessor and abbot.* Well, when St. Kevin had become celebrated for the sanctity

---

* He is supposed to have lived from 498 to 618, dying on June 3rd, which is his saint's day.

ST. NANNAN AND THE FLEAS. 177

of his life at Glendalough, a youth of noble birth, one of his pupils, happened to fall sick and had a great craving for apples. The saint in his sympathy offered up a prayer to the Lord for his relief, when a willow tree that grew near the church bore the wished-for fruit, which proved most beneficial not only to the lad but also to various ailing persons besides. And to this very day both that willow and sets planted from cuttings of it around the graveyard like an orchard produce apples every year, though in other respects, in their leaves and branches, they retain the peculiarities of the willow. These apples are light coloured and oblong in shape, and more wholesome than palatable. However, they are held in much veneration by the natives, who call them St. Kevin's apples; and many come from far distant parts of Ireland to fetch them as remedies for divers diseases.

Of the fleas which were banished by St. Nannan.
Girald. Cambr. Top. Hibern. Dis. II. cap. xxxi.

There is a village in Connaught, famed for a church dedicated to St. Nannan, where during many years swarms of fleas increased and multiplied to such an extent that the plague of it drove away almost all the inhabitants till every house was fairly deserted. At length St. Nannan came to their help, and the insects were banished to a neighbouring meadow. Nay, through the merits of that saint, so thoroughly did the Divine Power clear the place of the pest that not a flea could ever after be found there. But in the

M

meadow they continued to flourish and abound, insomuch that neither man nor even beast could ever enter it.

Of bells and staves and other similar relics of the saints.

Girald. Cambr. Top. Hibern. Dis. III. cap. xxxiii.

I should not omit to state also that portable bells, and the crooks of holy men of former times, curved at the upper end and wrought with gold, silver, or bronze, are held in deep reverence by both clergy and laity in Ireland and Scotland, as they are in Wales. So much so that oaths taken in the name of these relics are adhered to with far more fearful constancy than any sworn upon the holy Gospels. For by some occult power reposed in them, seemingly from above, and through that thirst for vengeance which characterizes the Irish saints, transgressors of such engagements are visited with the severest punishments.

Of that most potent relic known as the staff of Jesus; and how a priest was visited by a twofold affliction.

Girald. Cambr. Top. Hibern. Dis. III. cap. xxxiv.

Among all the crosiers of Ireland and wooden relics of the godly generally that which men call the staff of Jesus, of wide fame and rare virtue, stands out preeminent and deservedly holds the foremost place. It was by means of this, as the common belief goes, that St. Patrick ejected venomous snakes from the island.

The origin of the sacred rod is as uncertain as its miraculous properties are undoubted. The removal of the noble treasure from Armagh to Dublin was carried out in our day and by my own countrymen.*

I myself saw, too, in Wales, which made it all the more remarkable, a poor Irish beggar with a bronze-bound horn slung round his neck as a relic, and he averred that it had once belonged to Patrick. He added, moreover, that from awe of that holy saint no one had ever dared to wind it. But on his presenting the instrument to the bystanders to be kissed after the fashion of his country, one Bernard, a priest, snatched it out of his hand, and sticking it in the corner of his mouth blew into it and began to sound a blast. When immediately, in the sight of every one, he was struck with palsy, and his mouth was twisted right up to his ear. Indeed, he was doubly afflicted, for while he had previously been a man of fervid eloquence, though spiteful and malicious of tongue, he was reft on the spot of all power of speech. Full grievously was he smitten in this way, insomuch that he never wholly recovered, but has stammered ever since. Besides this, he sank into a kind of

* This celebrated crosier was encased in gold and adorned with gems. By its power St. Patrick was supposed to have been protected against all dangers, and we read of his using it wherewith to chastise the idols of the pagan Irish. The removal (by Fitz-Aldelm) of the relic to Dublin was probably for its safer keeping, and it continued to be preserved in Christ Church Cathedral and to be used in the ratification of treaties, etc. till it was publicly burnt in 1538 by a Protestant mob; but the precious metal and stones were removed first.

lethargy, and lost his faculty of recollection to such an extent that he could hardly remember his own name. In fact his memory was so affected that many days afterwards I saw him learning the psalms over again as if they were something absolutely fresh, although before his visitation he had known them perfectly by heart; and I marvelled to hear him, an old gray-headed man, stumbling over the first elements of learning, him whose erudition had been so wide.

At length he left home and went to Ireland to appeal to St. Patrick to heal his imbecility, and so was restored to somewhat better health, though never to what he had been at first.

Of the crucifix at Dublin which spoke and bore witness to the truth.

Girald. Cambr. Top. Dis. II. cap. xliv.

. . . At Dublin, in the church of the Holy Trinity, there is a certain cross, bearing the figure of the crucified Saviour, which is possessed of wondrous efficacy. Not many years before the coming of the English, that is to say in the days of the [supremacy of the] Ostmen [in that city], the effigy on this cross opened its sacred mouth and spoke. For it had happened that one of the citizens had invoked it as the sole witness and guarantee, as it were, of a contract. In course of time, however, he with whom he had entered into the agreement, broke the compact and persistently repudiated the loan, which had been granted on his personal security only. Their fellow-townsmen, therefore, proposed, ironically rather than in earnest, to lay the matter before the crucifix. Many persons assembled in the church to see the result, when, in the hearing of all, the figure, on being called upon, bore verbal witness to the truth.*

Of St. Colman's teal, which are tame and cannot be harmed.

Girald. Cambr. Top. Hibern. Dis. II. cap. xxix.

There is in Leinster a mere of no great size where dwell the birds of St. Colman : † that is small ducks, such as are commonly called teal. These since the time of the saint have been so tame that they will eat out of one's hand, and do not fear the approach of man. They are, too, always thirteen in number, as though forming a complete society.‡ If ever an injury is offered to the [neighbouring] church or clergy, or to them, or they are molested in any way, they immediately fly off and betake themselves to a far distant lake; and will not return to their home until condign punishment has overtaken the offender. Meanwhile, during their absence, the waters of their pool, which before were exquisitely pure and clear,

---

* This is the same crucifix as that mentioned in Book I. chap. 17 of the *Expugnatio*.

† Sometime bishop of Lindisfarne, and afterwards founder of the monastery of Inisbofinne in Connamara. Died 674, on August 8th, which is his day.

‡ The prior and his twelve monks, or the prioress and her twelve nuns, the original nucleus of a religious society.

become foul and fetid and fit to be used by neither men nor cattle.

At times it has occurred that some one fetching water thence at night has, not intentionally but accidentally, drawn up one of the little creatures in his bucket, and after his supper has been on the fire a long time without properly cooking, at last the bird has been found swimming about in the pot perfectly unhurt; while as soon as it has been restored to the pool, the meat has been cooked at once.

It came to pass, also, in our days that as Robert Fitz-Stephen and Dermot, king of Leinster, were marching by that spot an archer brought down one of these fowl with an arrow. He took it off with him to his quarters, and put it in a vessel with some flesh to boil, yet though he spent as much wood over it as would be enough for three fires and waited till midnight he got no farther with his cooking: the pot would not boil. Three times he took the meat out, and each time it was just as raw as it had been at first. At length his host spied the little duck among the pieces of flesh, and on hearing that it had come from the pool, burst into tears and exclaimed: 'Woe is me, that ever such a mischance as this should happen in my house! Why, this was one of St. Colman's teal!' And the victuals on being placed upon the fire alone were straightway boiled without difficulty. But the archer soon after perished miserably.

Besides, it came about that a kite seized one of them, and perched with it on a neighbouring tree, when forthwith in the presence of many beholders, he was stricken with a rigidity in all his limbs, and paid no further regard to the victim he held in his talons. So, too, one winter, another was carried off by a young fox; and in the morning the beast was discovered near the mere, lying dead in a hut, sacred from its having formerly been the resort of St. Colman. His prey had stuck in his throat and choked him.

In all the above cases the birds, through the kindly care of their excellent patron, returned to the pool uninjured, while the spoilers paid the penalty of death.

Of the archers at Finglas who were punished by Heaven.

Girald. Cambr. Top. Hibern. Dis. II. cap. liv.

It fell out, also, in our days that during the unusually violent storms in Ireland, while Jove rent the heavens with his thunder,* and while the sword of king Henry flashed lightning through the land, several companies of archers happened to be quartered in Finglas, a village belonging to the archbishop of Dublin. These fellows at once proceeded in a grossly irreverent way to lay violent hands upon the ashes, yews, and various trees which the famous abbot Chenach and other devout men by whose constant piety the spot is glorified had in times gone by planted with their own hands around the grave-yard to adorn their church. For, although there was a wood near by, with the usual depraved manners of the baser sort

* Gerald, *Expug.* I. 36.

added to the customary license of soldiers, they attacked these trees, and lopping some, tearing up others root and branch, soon consumed almost all in their fires. . . .

But through the just indignation of God, who claims vengeance as His own, and deigns to take upon Himself the punishment even in this life of injuries offered to His saints, these rude bowmen were forthwith smitten so sorely with a strange and sudden pestilence that within a few days most of them died a wretched death in that very village; suffering by the decision of a strict Judge in that court which had seen their sin. The rest of them essayed to find refuge on ship-board, but were wrecked and drowned, and thus found in their extremity that the same Lord is ruler of the sea as of the land; that from His face no man can escape, or even flee.

Of various miracles in Kildare; and first of the fire that never goes out, and the ashes which do not increase.

Girald. Cambr. Top. Hibern. Dis. II. cap. xxxiv.

At Kildare, in Leinster, a town rendered illustrious by the glorious Bridget,* are many marvels well worthy of relation. Among these the first that occurs to my mind is her fire, which men say never dies. Not that it cannot be extinguished, but because nuns and holy women have ever fed the flames with fuel and cherished them with such anxious and careful diligence that

* The Irish form is "Brighit," "the fiery dart."

through the whole course of years from the time of the virgin [Bridget] they have always remained burning. And for all the quantity of wood that must have been consumed during so long a period, yet the ash-heap has not increased.

How the fire is kept up by Bridget herself on her own night.

Girald. Cambr. Top. Hibern. Dis. II. cap. xxxv.

As in the days of Bridget twenty nuns served the Lord here, she herself being one of the twenty, since her translation into heaven nineteen have invariably formed the society down to the present time, and no addition has ever been made to that number. Each of them in turn watches the fire for a night, and on the twentieth evening the nun last on duty, after piling up the logs, says : ' Bridget, look to your hearth : it is your night.' And so the fire is left, yet in the morning it is found still blazing, and the usual amount of wood has been burnt.

Concerning the hedge set around the fire, within which no male may go.

Girald. Cambr. Top. Hibern. Dis. II. cap. xxxvi.

This fire is surrounded by a circular hedge of stakes and brushwood, within which no male may enter. And if perchance any such dare to pass it, and certain rash men have essayed to do so, they will not escape the Divine vengeance.

Moreover, it is lawful for women alone to blow it up, and these may not do so with the breath of their mouths, but with bellows only or with fans.

Of an archer who leapt over St. Bridget's hedge and went raving mad; and of another who lost the use of his leg.

Girald. Cambr. Top. Hibern. Dis. II. cap. xlviii.

At Kildare an archer of the household of earl Richard leapt over the hedge and blew the fire of St. Bridget with his mouth. But no sooner had he jumped back again than he was seized with madness, and ran about blowing into the mouth of every one he met, saying: 'See! this is how I blew St. Bridget's fire!' In the same way, too, he rushed in and out of the houses over the whole town, and whenever he saw a fire, repeated the same words and blew at it. At last, however, he was caught by his comrades and tied down, whereupon he begged to be taken to the nearest water; and on being led thither, in his burning thirst, drank so huge a quantity that he burst with a loud report in the midst of them, and expired in their hands.

Another, also, who wanted to get at the fire, had just stretched one leg over the hedge, when, although he was dragged back and held fast by his companions, the offending foot and limb were forthwith withered up, and for the rest of his life he continued lame, and an idiot as well.

ST. KEVIN AND THE BLACKBIRD. 187

That the saints of this land appear to be of a vindictive disposition.

Girald. Cambr. Top. Hibern. Dis. II. cap. lv.

This, too, seems to me deserving of note, that even as the men of the Irish nation are in this mortal life beyond all others passionate and quick to revenge, so in the life after death the saints of the island, exalted though they be by their virtues above those of other countries, appear to be of a vengeful temper.

The only reason I can think of for this is that the people of Ireland, having no castles, while their land swarms with robbers, are wont (especially the ecclesiastics) in the absence of fortified places to seek refuge and protection for themselves and their goods in the churches. Whence, by the permission of Divine Providence it has often been found necessary to inflict chastisement upon such as may have assaulted sacred buildings. Whereby both the peace o f the church was guarded from the hands of the impious, and not merely a befitting but even a servile veneration was secured for the holy edifices themselves on the part of a race naturally irreverent.

[Of St. Kevin's gentleness.]

Girald. Cambr. Top. Hibern. Dis. II. cap. xxviii.

Once during Lent St. Kevin, as was his wont at that season, fled from intercourse with man to a desert place,* where, sheltered only by a little hut which was

---
* In the valley of Glendalough.

just sufficient to keep off the sun and rain, he gave himself up to holy meditation and passed his time in reading and in prayer. One day when, as usual, he raised his hand to heaven through the window, a blackbird chanced to settle on it, and treating the palm as a nest laid her eggs there. The good man, struck with compassion, showed such patience and gentleness that he neither closed his hand nor drew it in; but hollowed it and continued to hold it out without wearying till the young brood was fully hatched. And in lasting memory of this remarkable incident all the images of St. Kevin throughout Ireland bear a blackbird in the extended hand.

Of the wonderful sanctuaries provided by the saints.

Girald. Cambr. Top. Hibern. Dis. II. cap. xl.

In further Ulster rise some mountains where cranes and grouse and various other birds build in large numbers during their season, for the sake of the peaceful asylum there afforded not only to human beings, but to brutes and to the fowls of the air as well. There all such abide undisturbed by the inhabitants owing to the respect for St. Bean,* whose church dignifies the spot. That saint, besides pro-

---

* An Irishman of this name was appointed first bishop of Aberdeen in 1010, and is commemorated upon December 16th. But perhaps the saint here is Binen, or Benignus, archbishop of Armagh, St. Patrick's disciple and successor in the primacy, whose day is November 9th.

tecting his birds, also watches over their eggs in a wondrous and unheard-of way. For directly you stretch out your arm to seize them, they disappear and you see in their place a brood of young chicks, red and scraggy, as though hatched that very hour. You naturally draw back your hand, and, lo, you behold in turn, through either some miracle or some optical illusion, the chicks transformed again in a surprising manner into eggs. If two persons go, one to look on while the other robs the nest, to the eyes of the latter appear chicks, to those of the former eggs.

In South Munster, between the hill of Brendan * and the wide sea which flows between Spain and Ireland, lies a region of some extent, bounded on one side by a river that teems with fish, on the other by a small stream. There, out of reverence for St. Brendan and other saints of that part, is a wondrous refuge for men, cattle, and even for savage beasts, whether indigenous to the locality or such as have migrated thither from elsewhere. Whence it is that stags, wild boars, hares, and other animals of the chase, on finding they can in no wise escape from the hounds that are close upon their track, make with all speed for this district from far distant quarters. And when they have once passed the rivulet, the dogs stop short in the pursuit at that moment, and the fugitive is immediately safe from all danger.

Marvellous is the power of God, who through the merits of His saints does not permit the persistent and

* Brandon Hill, in Kerry.

cruel huntsman to secure his prey, though he vehemently urge on his fierce dogs to drag down the quarry that is perhaps but a few yards ahead.

In these two retreats, from long enjoyment of a home-like repose, birds and untamed animals do not flee from intercourse with man.

On the other side of the said tract of land runs a river which abounds in fish, and is especially rich in salmon, even to an astonishing degree. This great plenty was bestowed by Providence in the cause of charity; for the purpose, that is, of supplying plentiful material for that indefatigable hospitality which the holy men there were accustomed to afford to pilgrims and strangers to the utmost of their power, indeed far more than they ought in justice to themselves. And lest the too common greed of man should be tempted to turn this same abundance to marketable account, a remedy has been provided which resembles that of the manna: for never will these fish keep a single night after their taking. Though they be salted as thoroughly as possible, they are always liable to turn putrid, and remain tasteless and insipid; nor can they by any device be preserved till the morrow so as to be of the slightest value as an eatable.

Of the salmon leap.

Girald. Cambr. Top. Hibern. Dis. II. cap. xli.

This river, too, pours over and down a natural rock, where it falls with great force from the top to the bottom, forming a cascade such as one often sees.

On the summit of the waterfall is a hole of moderate size, scooped out ages ago by the hands of holy men. Into this cavity great numbers of the salmon bound from below with a wonderful leap: one, in fact, which would be miraculous were not this the peculiar habit of that fish, for the height is as much as the length of the longest spear.* Hence the name salmon has been given to this species owing to its native propensity to saltation.

How the salmon leap.

Girald. Cambr. Top. Hibern. Dis. II. cap. xlii.

The particular mode in which they leap is as follows. Fishes of this sort struggle by instinct up stream: they strive against the current as birds do against the blast. When a precipitous obstacle comes in their path, they bend their tails round towards their heads; and sometimes, to give greater elasticity to their spring, even take them fast in their mouths. Then they suddenly let go, and relax the kind of circle thus made, and, like the jerk of a bowed rod when abruptly released, with the impetus so gained throw themselves to the wonder of the spectators a great height from the base to the top of whatever bars their way.

A leap similar to this one, though not so large, is to be seen in the river Liffey, not far from Dublin.†

* About twelve feet, at that time.

† Leixlip: the word is Norse and means "salmon-leap." "Lax" occurs in various place names in Scotland, the isles, and Ireland.

In the Teivy, too, in South Wales, is a third, which is the steepest of the three.

> That the bodies of S.S. Patrick, Columba, and Bridget, which lay at the city of Down in Ulster, were in these our days discovered and translated.
>
> *Girald. Cambr. Top. Hibern.* Dis. III. cap. xviii.

Now contemporaneous * with St. Patrick had been S.S. Columba and Bridget, and the remains of all three had been interred in the same city, that is Down. In our own times, in the year in which the lord John first came into Ireland [1185], and during the governorship of John de Courci in Ulster, these noble treasures were, through the instrumentality of the latter, translated. Their burial-place was revealed by divine agency, and the bodies were found in a vault with three recesses, St. Patrick lying in the middle, the others on either side.†

* Not correct, as the dates given above will show.

† The revelation was made in a vision to the bishop of Down, and on June 9th (St. Columkille's day), 1186, the remains were solemnly *translated* to a monument in Downpatrick Cathedral in the presence of the legate Vivianus and a large gathering of the Irish clergy.

> "In Down three saints one tomb do fill,
> "Patrick, Bridget, and Columkille."
>
> (*Quoted by Connellan*).

GENEALOGICAL TABLES OF THE GERALDINES AND THEIR CONQUEST OF IRE

A. Legitimate descendants of the princess Nesta, daughter of Rhys ap Griffith, all successively

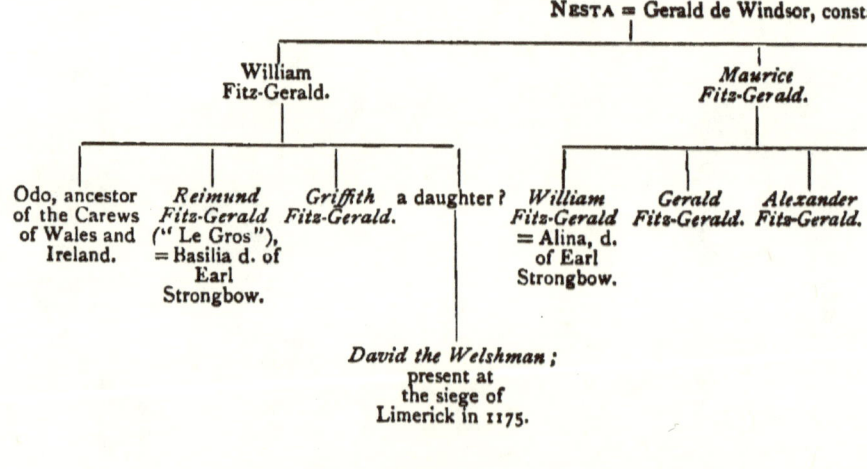

NESTA = Gerald de Windsor, const

├── William Fitz-Gerald.
│   ├── Odo, ancestor of the Carews of Wales and Ireland.
│   ├── Reimund Fitz-Gerald ("Le Gros"), = Basilia d. of Earl Strongbow.
│   └── Griffith Fitz-Gerald.
│   └── a daughter?
│   └── David the Welshman; present at the siege of Limerick in 1175.
└── Maurice Fitz-Gerald.
    ├── William Fitz-Gerald = Alina, d. of Earl Strongbow.
    ├── Gerald Fitz-Gerald.
    └── Alexander Fitz-Gerald.

B. Descent from the princess Nesta, which

NESTA = Stephen,
│
Robert Fitz-Stephen
│
Ralph Fitz-Stephen [certainly illegitimate]
= d. of Milo de Cogan.

C. Descent from the princess Nesta, which

NESTA = Henry I.,
│
Fitz-Henry [certainly illegitima
├── Meiler Fitz-Henry [legitimate] = N——, d. of Hugh de Laci.
└── Robert Fitz-Henry [legitim

N.B.—1. The order of seniority among the brothers and sisters is in some cases dou

APPENDIX I.

... AND THEIR KINSMEN, THE FIRST ADVENTURERS IN THE ... OF IRELAND.

..., daughter of Rhys ap Tudor, sister of Griffith, and aunt ... ...ccessively princes of South Wales:—

... Windsor, constable of Pembroke.

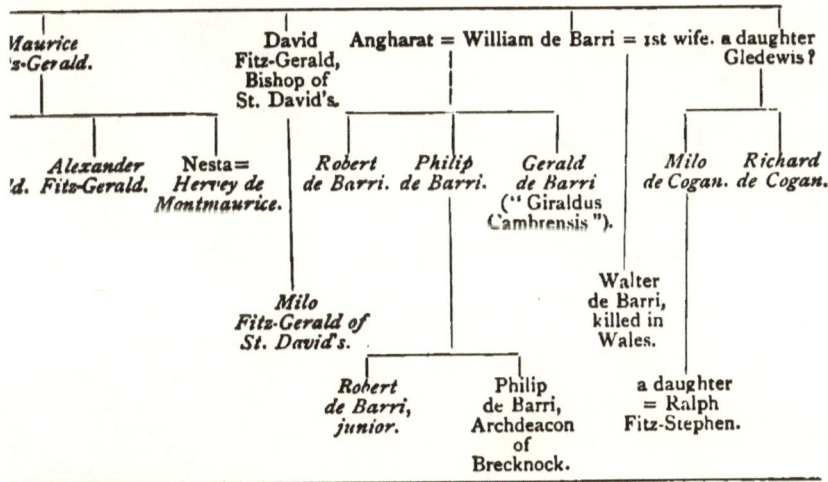

..sta, which was probably illegitimate:—

...ESTA = Stephen, constable of Cardigan.

...rt Fitz-Stephen [probably illegitimate].

Meredith Fitz-Stephen [certainly illegitimate].

sta, which was certainly illegitimate:—

...TA = Henry I., King of England.

...rtainly illegitimate].

..-Henry [legitimate].   Henry Fitz-Henry [legitimate?].

in some cases doubtful.   2. Those in *italics* took part in the conquest.

APPENDIX II.

A LIST OF THE MOST PROMINENT PERSONS CONCERNED IN THE CONQUEST OF IRELAND UNDER HENRY II.

A. Adventurers.

Richard de Clare, Earl of Pembroke or Strigul ["*Strongbow*"].
Maurice Fitz-Gerald.
Reimund Fitz-Gerald.
Griffith Fitz-Gerald.
William Fitz-Gerald.
Gerald Fitz-Gerald.
Alexander Fitz-Gerald.
Milo Fitz-Gerald, of St. David's.
Hervey de Montmaurice.
Robert de Barri.
Philip de Barri.
Robert de Barri, junior.
Milo de Cogan [*Cogham*].
Richard de Cogan.
Robert Fitz-Stephen.
Ralph Fitz-Stephen.
Meredith Fitz-Stephen.
Meiler Fitz-Henry.
Robert Fitz-Henry.
Henry Fitz-Henry.
Reimund de Kantitune.
Reimund Fitz-Hugh.
Walter de Ridenesford.
Maurice de Prendergast.
William Mascarel.
Philip of Wales [*Gualensis*].
Richard Fitz-Godobert.
Alice de [A]berveny.
Robert de Quency.

Richard de Marreis.
Walter Bluet.
John de Clahull.
Robert de Birmingham.
Adam de Hereford.
John de Hereford.
Thomas de Flanders [*le Fleming*].
Robert de Bigarz.
Simon de Bigarz.
Robert de Borard.
Hugh Tyrell [*The Earl's "intrinsicke friend;" Carew*].
William the Little ["*Petit ;*" "*Modicus*"].
Gilbert de Nangle.
Josselin Fitz-Gilbert.
Richard Tuite.
Robert de Laci.
Richard de la Chappell.
Geoffrey de Constantin.
Adam de Feipo.
Gilbert de Nugent.
William de Muset.
Hugh de Hosé.
Adam Dullard.
Richard le Fleming.
Adam de Riceport.
Robert Fitz-Richard.

B. Left behind or sent over by the king in various official capacities.

Prince John, *as Lord of Ireland*.
William Fitz-Aldelm, *as Procurator*.
Robert Fitz-Barnard.
Hugh de Laci, *as Procurator*.
John de Courci, *as coadjutor to Fitz-Aldelm ; then as chief governor under John*.
Humphrey de Bohun.
Bertram de Verdun.

Robert le Poer [*le pauvre*].
William le Poer.
Roger le Poer.
Osbert de Herlotera.
William de Bendenges.
Adam de Yarmouth.
Philip de Braose.
Philip de Worcester, *as Procurator*.
Theobald Fitz-Walter.
John Constable of Chester, } *as temporary co-governors.*
Richard de Pec,
Hugh de Gundeville.
Philip de Hastings.
Gilbert de Boisrohard.
Reimund de Drune.
Hubert Fitz-Hubert.
William Fitz-Hubert.
Joslan de la Pumerai.
Richard de Londres.

Ecclesiastics. { Robert of Shrewsbury, *to watch Hugh de Laci for the King.*
John Comyn, *as Archbishop of Dublin.*
Gerald de Barri ["*Cambrensis*"], *as adviser to Prince John.*

C. Sent by the pope.

Vivianus, *as Papal legate.*

APPENDIX III.

A LIST OF THE LEADING IRISH AND NORSE CHIEFTAINS AND NOTABLES WHO APPEAR DURING THE WAR.

A. Irishmen.

Roderic, King of Connaught and High-King of all Ireland.
Dermot Mac Murrough, King of Leinster.
Cooley Mac Donlevy, King of Ulidia.
Roderic Mac Donlevy, King of Ulidia.
Dermot Mac Carthy, King of Desmond [*aliter* S. Munster, *aliter* Cork].
Donnell O'Brien, King of Thomond [*aliter* N. Munster, *aliter* Limerick].
Donnell, King of Ossory.
Tiernan O'Ruarc, King of Breifny and East Meath.
Mackelan, Prince of Ophelan.
Murtough Mac Murrough, Prince of Hy-Kinselagh [Kenceleia].
Melaghlin O'Phelan, Prince of Decies.
Melaghlin O'Neill, King of Keneleonia.
Murrough O'Carroll, King of Uriel.
Donnell Kevanagh, son of Dermot, King of Leinster.
Awelaph [Anlaf] O'Carvi.
O'Reilli of Tirbrun.
} The only Irish chiefs who continued to stand by the English after the death of Dermot Mac Murrough.

Ecclesiastics. {
[St.] Gelasius, Archbishop of Armagh and Primate of all Ireland.
[St.] Lawrence O'Toole, Archbishop of Dublin.
Donatus, Archbishop of Cashel.
Catholicus, Archbishop of Tuam.
Christian, Bishop of Lismore and Papal legate.
}

B. Ostmen.

Reginald of Waterford.
Smorch of Waterford.

The two Sihtrics of Waterford.
Hasculf of Dublin.
John the Wood ["le Devé;" *Regan*].
Guthred, King of Man.

APPENDIX IV.

THE IRISH EPISCOPATE AT THE TIME OF THE INVASION.

From Hoveden, sub anno 1171.

Metropolitan Archbishoprick of Armagh.

Suffragan Bishopricks.—Kells, Louth (Clogher), Down, Derry, Raphoe, Connor, Ardagh, Clonard.

Archbishoprick of Cashel.

Suffragan · Bishopricks.—Lismore, Emly, Cloyne, Ardmore, Limerick, Killaloe, Waterford, Ardfert, Ross, Kilfenora.*

Archbishoprick of Dublin.

Suffragan Bishopricks.—Glendalough, Ferns, Leighlin, Kildare, Ossory.

Archbishoprick of Tuam.

Suffragan Bishopricks.—Clonfert, Killala, Mayo, Elphin, Achonry.

---

* Benedict Abbas, I. 27, adds Cork.

APPENDIX V.

ELUCIDATION OF THE MAP.

The five great divisions mentioned by Gerald in Bk. I., chap. 1, of the "Expugnatio Hibernica," and forming the *Irish Pentarchy*, were Leinster, Munster, Connaught, Ulster, and Meath. Of these—

Leinster = the modern counties of Wexford, Carlow, Wicklow, and Queen's County, most of Kilkenny, King's County, and Kildare, and the southern half of the county of Dublin.

Munster = the modern province exactly, together with part of Kilkenny.

Connaught = the modern province exactly, with the addition of the greater part of Cavan.

Ulster = as now, but with Louth and without Cavan, except a small district in the east of the latter county.

Meath = the modern counties of Meath and West Meath, with parts of Longford, King's County, and Kildare, and the northern half of the county of Dublin.

Other districts—

In Leinster—Kenceleia = the diocese of Ferns, *i.e.* roughly the modern county of Wexford.

,, ,, —Ossory = the diocese of Ossory, *i.e.* most of Kilkenny and part of Queen's County, the latter portion being sub-named Leix.

,, ,, —Offaly = N. Kildare and parts of King's and Queen's counties.

,, ,, —Omorethi = S. Kildare.

,, ,, —Odrone = part of W. Carlow.

EXPLANATION OF THE MAP. 201

In **Munster** —Thomond = roughly Clare and Limerick counties.

„ „ —Desmond = Cork, Kerry, Waterford, and S. Tipperary counties. Minor divisions in Desmond were Olethan in S.E. of co. Cork, and the Decies in co. Waterford; though they are sometimes reckoned as districts independent of Desmond.

„ „ —Ormond = N.W. Tipperary.

In **Connaught**—Breifny = Leitrim and Cavan counties.

In **Ulster** —Uriel = Louth, Armagh, Monaghan and most of Fermanagh counties.

„ „ —Ulidia = Antrim and Down counties, the latter being sub-named Dalaradia.

„ „ —Keneleonia = Londonderry and Tyrone counties.

„ „ —Tirconnel = co. Donegal.

CHIEF PLACES OF IMPORTANCE AND INTEREST IN IRELAND AT THE TIME OF THE CONQUEST.

Dublin.*
Wexford.*
Waterford or Port Lairge.*
Cork.
Limerick.*
Down.

Tuam.
Armagh.
Cashel.
Ferns.
Lismore.
Leighlin.
Tara.

Carlingford.*
Louth.
Wicklow.*
Arklow.*
Kildare.

* Ostman settlements.

APPENDIX VI.

THE AUTHORITIES.

1. GERALD DE BARRI, known in literature as Silvester Giraldus Cambrensis, the historian of the conquest of Ireland and a member of the family which furnished the chief leaders during the first years of the invasion, was born, about 1147, at his father's castle of Manorbier in Pembrokeshire, near Tenby. He was of gentle birth, and by descent half Anglo-Norman half Welsh [*see Genealogical Table*]. A younger son, and destined for the church, he received his education partly from his uncle, David Fitz-Gerald, bishop of St. David's, partly at the University of Paris, which was already showing signs of its coming greatness as the chief centre of European learning. In 1176 Bishop David died, and the chapter elected Gerald, who had been archdeacon of Brecknock for the last four years, to succeed him. The young archdeacon, however, had already earned the reputation of being a restless advocate of church reform; he was known to be a zealous upholder of the claims of St. David's to independence of Canterbury; finally the preferment of a Welshman to the metropolitan see of Wales was regarded as dangerous: for these reasons the king refused his consent to the appointment. In disgust, Gerald returned to Paris, where he passed the next four years in study. It was in February 1183 that he paid his first visit to Ireland, and there remained for about a year assisting his relatives with advice (*Expug*. II. 20). His connection with the court seems to have begun in 1184, when Henry, who had made his acquaintance in South Wales, enlisted his services as a diplomatist in Welsh affairs. He was also appointed a royal chaplain and tutor to prince John, whom he accompanied to Ireland in 1185 (*Expug*. II. 32). More than once an Irish bishoprick was offered to him, but the ambition of his life was to be bishop of St. David's, and from that aim he would not turn aside. By the spring of 1188 the *Topographia* was published, and about twelve months later the *Expugnatio*. Some time after the

completion of the former work, the writer's vanity was gratified by his spending three days at Oxford in publicly reciting it, and feasting everybody, high and low. The *Topographia* he dedicated to Henry II., and the *Expugnatio* to Richard I. when count of Poitou. Of his other works it is unnecessary to speak here. On Richard I.'s departure for the East in 1189, Gerald was appointed by the king a member of the council of regency, and his hopes of obtaining the see of St. David's revived ; so much so that he declined the bishopricks of Bangor and Llandaff, though they might have seemed steps to the coveted post. Yet when in 1198 St. David's again fell vacant, and Gerald was a second time chosen by the chapter, Archbishop Hubert Walter, who was justiciar of the realm in the absence of the king, set aside the election for the same considerations as those which had caused its repudiation before ; and we can quite imagine that our author was a man who in high office might have been a great nuisance. While the matter was still open, Richard died and John succeeded. A long dispute now began, during which an appeal was made to the pope. Finally, in 1203, Gerald withdrew from the contest, and soon after retired into private life, a disappointed man. We only hear of him again as going on a pilgrimage to Rome in 1205-6, and as sullenly rejecting the tardy offer of St. David's in 1214. His death took place apparently in 1220, but he had so dropped out of the world that the exact year is not certain.

St. David's had originally been the seat of the primacy of Wales, and the succession of archbishops practically went on from St. David, about 519, till the time of Bishop Bernard, 1115-47, who submitted to the supremacy of Canterbury. David Fitz-Gerald, who followed him, began the list of bishops subordinate to the English primate. Gerald had given much offence to king John by defending before pope Innocent III. in 1199 the ancient metropolitan rights of the extinct archbishoprick.*

The literary vagaries of Gerald and his merits as a writer of

---

* Among the works of Hubert Walter, archbishop of Canterbury, was one entitled *A Censure of Gerald at Rome.*

history have been touched upon in the preface. Sufficient was said there to place the reader on his guard against accepting with implicit confidence all that he would find in the extracts from the *Expugnatio*. The author's attitude to the Irish resembles that of Bernal Diaz to the Mexicans. Yet partial though his narrative is to his own countrymen, it is perhaps not more unjust to the natives than it is to most of the royal officers who were sent over to counteract the influence of his kinsmen the Geraldines. Still, when all is said, the *Expugnatio* remains beyond comparison the most complete and detailed account of the expedition; so we must be grateful, if not content. And the very extravagance of Gerald's faults as a historian is their corrective: were he less obviously unfair, he would be the more delusive.

2. *The Annals of the kingdom of Ireland by the Four Masters* from the earliest period to the year 1616 were compiled between January 22nd, 1632 and August 10th, 1636 in the convent of Donegal, from Old Irish Annals, most of the original MSS. of which are now lost. The work is dedicated to Fergal O'Gara, lord of Moy O'Gara and Coolavin, in co. Sligo, who patronized the undertaking and paid the antiquaries engaged in the task, while the convent housed and fed them. The Four Masters were Michael O'Clery, Conary O'Clery, Cucogry O'Clery, and Ferfeasa O'Mulconry. They did not themselves assume the appellation of the Four Masters; the title was given to them afterwards, and was suggested by the designation *Quatuor Magistri*, "applied by medical writers of the middle ages to the Four Masters of the medical sciences" (O'Donovan). The Annals are written in Goidelic, and the selections are from the translation of O'Donovan published in 1851, as also are those from the Annals of Innisfallen, which are quoted in his notes.

On the whole considerably less is said in the Four Masters about the English invasion than might have been expected: indeed the excerpts here given comprise practically all the connected pieces of interest on the subject; though there are short entries besides from time to time. The rest consists at this period mainly of the record of a network of "predatory incursions," feuds, usurpations, depositions, and assassinations, which apparently go on as usual with undiminished vigour in the presence of the invader: the internecine strife being but rarely suspended, and only during some few brief and spasmodic coalitions against the foreigners.

3. The *Annals of Innisfallen*, from the creation to the year A.D. 1320, were composed at the monastery on the isle of Innisfallen in the lake of Killarney. They are believed to have been begun about A.D. 1000, and are in the Goidelic tongue with an intermixture of Latin.

4. The *Annals of Loch Cé*, or, more correctly, the "Annals of the Rock of Loch Cé," or, the "Annals of Carrick ('Crag') Maç Dermot," were compiled at the old home of the Mac Dermots on an island in lough Key in Roscommon. They embrace the period between the battle of Clontarf (1014) and 1590, and in their extant shape were partly the work of Brian Mac Dermot, who died in 1592. They are probably the family record of the Mac Dermots combined with transcripts from other annals. The language is Goidelic with occasional Latin sentences.

5. The *Annals of Boyle*, in Roscommon, were carried on by the monks of the abbey of that place. They cover the time from 420 to 1245, and are written in Goidelic interspersed with a considerable proportion of Latin.

6. The *Annals of Clonmacnoise*, from Adam to Henry IV. inclusive. The original Goidelic of these Annals is not known to be in existence, and the only version of them extant is an English translation. There are but three MS. copies of this, and it has never been printed. The translation was made in 1627, by Connla Mac Echagan [Mageoghegan]. One of the copies is in the Clarendon Collection in the British Museum, the press-mark being Ayscough, 4817. The MS. is written in Elizabethan style, and in a bold and legible hand.

7. The *Annals of Ulster* were originally compiled by Cathal Mac Guire at his isle of Senait in lough Erne. They start from A.D. 431, and go on to 1498, on March 23rd of which year the

writer died of small-pox aged 59. His work was taken up by Roderic Cassidy, and continued by him to 1541, and subsequently by others till 1604. There is a translation into English by an unknown person of the early part down to 1303, preserved in the Clarendon Collection at the British Museum, Ayscough, 4795. This MS. is in a crabbed hand of the seventeenth century, and is frequently difficult to decipher. The translation has not been printed.

8. The *Anglo-Norman poem on the conquest of Ireland by Henry Ii.* is the production of an unknown rimer, who, as he tells us, drew his information chiefly from Morice Regan, the interpreter or secretary (*Latinier, Latimer*) of Dermot, king of Leinster. Besides the oral account he obtained from Regan, the poet was also furnished by him with another *geste*, or song, on the invasion, which is not known to be in existence. To these sources of knowledge he added the reminiscences of old men and others. It is impossible to say whether the poem was composed before or after the *Expugnatio* of Gerald. In the latter case it is difficult to believe that the author had not read, if he did not make use of, so celebrated a work as that of de Barri. His referring to old men as constituting one class of his authorities would perhaps point to its being subsequent in date to the *Expugnatio*. From what has been said, however, it is clear that the poet lived during or near the time of the occurrences of which he sings. His story breaks off suddenly at the attack on Limerick by Reimund in 1175. On the whole it agrees very well with Gerald's history, although each narrative contains facts and incidents which are wanting in the other. The verses are constructed in heptasyllabic couplets, varied occasionally by octo-syllabic lines, but with further irregularities of metre here and there. The text, which is very corrupt, was edited by Michel and Wright in 1837. As Mr. Dimock remarks (Preface to Vol. 5 of Giraldus Cambrensis, R.S.) this was just such a *chanson de geste* as would be chanted in many a Norman castle hall of a winter's night at the end of the xiith century.

In Harris's *Hibernica*, 1747, was printed an imperfect abstract of this poem in English prose made by sir George Carew, lord president of Munster in the reign of Elizabeth, and a descendant of the Geraldines [*see Genealogical Table*]. Until the publication of the Anglo-Norman text in 1837, this abstract was always taken as equivalent to the original, which, being extant in a single MS., was not easy to consult. Two passages from Carew's epitome have been inserted in this book under the year 1169, a comparison with the poem having shown them to be sufficiently accurate to justify their being so utilized. Carew believed Regan to have been the actual author of the *geste*, hence that fragment has been generally known and quoted as "Regan." *

9. The English authorities in Latin used besides the above-mentioned works of Gerald of Barri are *The Chronicles of Roger of Howden* (732-1201); *The Deeds of King Henry II.*, ascribed to Benedict, abbot of Peterborough, but probably written by the king's treasurer, Richard Fitz-Neal, the author of the "Dialogus de Scaccario," (1169-1192); *The Outlines of History* by Ralph of Dissay, dean of St. Paul's, (1147-1201); *The History of English Affairs* by William of Newbury (1066-1198); The *Chronicles* of Robert, abbot of St. Michael's Mount, (876-1184); The *Chronicle* of Gervase of Canterbury, (1122-1200); The *Chronicle* of Ralph Niger (creation to 1199); *The Kingdom of the Britons from Brute to* 1210 by Gervase of Tilbury; † *The Archives of Dublin;* and a MS. on vellum preserved in the British Museum, Clarendon Collection, Ayscough, 4792, labelled *A genuine copy of an ancient charter granted by Hugh de Laci to William the Little.*

---

* I must not omit to say that my thanks are due to my friend and late colleague, J. Russell Esq. M.A., who rendered me kind and valuable assistance in dealing with the difficult text of this poem, although he is in no way responsible for the translation.

† Of these Roger of Howden, Fitz-Neal, and Ralph of Dissay were all in the service of Henry II., while William of Newbury and Robert of St. Michael's Mount also had special facilities for obtaining information.

10. I have also consulted *The Martyrology of Donegal*, by Michael O'Clery, the senior of the Four Masters; Colgan's *Deeds of the Irish Saints;* The *Syllabus of Rymer's Foedera;* The *Calendar of Documents relating to Ireland;* Spencer's *View of the State of Ireland*, written in 1596; Hanmer's *Chronicle of Ireland*, written in 1571; Campion's *History of Ireland*, written in 1571: and must acknowledge my indebtedness to O'Curry's *Lectures on the MS. Materials of Ancient Irish History*, O'Curry's *Manners and Customs of the Ancient Irish*, O'Clery's Edition of the *Four Masters*, and that by Connellan and Mac Dermott, Mr. Round's articles on John de Courci, Kelly's *Calendar of Irish Saints*, the "Index Locorum" in O'Donovan's Edition of *The Four Masters*, and to the Glossary in Vol. V of the Rolls Edition of *Giraldus Cambrensis*.

LIST OF EDITIONS USED.

Giraldi Cambrensis Topographia Hibernica et Expugnatio Hibernica: ed. Dimock; R.S. [*Rolls Series*].
Chronica Magistri Rogeri de Houedene: ed. Stubbs; R.S.
Gesta Regis Henrici Secundi Benedicti Abbatis: ed. Stubbs; R.S.
Radulphi de Diceto Decani Lundoniensis Ymagines Historiarum: ed. Stubbs; R.S.
Historia Rerum Anglicarum Wilelmi Newburgensis: ed. Howlett; R.S.
Gervasii Monachi Cantuariensis Opera Historica: ed. Stubbs; R.S.
Chronica Roberti Abbatis S. Michaelis de Monte, in Vol. 6 of the "Monumenta Germaniæ Historica" of Pertz.
Chronicon Radulphi Nigri, cum continuatione per anonymum, in Vol. 27 of the "Monumenta Germaniæ Historica" of Pertz.
Excerpta ex otiis Imperialibus Gervasii Tileburiensis: ed. Stevenson; R.S.
The Archives of the City of Dublin: ed. Gilbert; R.S.
Annales Buelliani, in the "Rerum Hibernicarum Scriptores Veteres:" ed. O'Conor, 1814.

LIST OF EDITIONS. 209

An Anglo-Norman Poem on the Conquest of Ireland by Henry II. : ed. Michel and Thomas Wright, Pickering, 1837.
Maurice Regan's History of Ireland: Trans. [in abstract] by Carew, 1757.
The Annals of the Kingdom of Ireland by the Four Masters: Trans. and ed. O'Donovan.
The Annals of Innisfallen (from the notes in the above).
The Annals of Loch Cé : ed. and trans. Hennessy ; R.S.
The Annals of Ireland : ed. O'Clery.
The Annals of Ireland : Trans. and ed. Connellan and Mac Dermott.
The Syllabus of Rymer's Fœdera : ed. Hardy, Record Edition.
The Martyrology of Donegal by Michael O'Clery : Irish Archæological Society.
Acta Sanctorum Hiberniæ by Colgan : Louvain, 1645.
The Irish Histories of Spencer, Campion, Hanmer, and Marleborrough : Dublin, 1809.
The Calendar of Documents relating to Ireland : ed. Sweetman ; R.S.

www.ingramcontent.com/pod-product-compliance
Lightning Source LLC
Chambersburg PA
CBHW021825230426
43669CB00008B/871